AN AFGHAN HOUND

DOGS
OF CHARACTER

Written and Illustrated by

Cecil Aldin

DOVER PUBLICATIONS, INC., Mineola, New York

Bibliographical Note

Dogs of Character, first published by Dover Publications, Inc., in 2013, is a republication of the work originally published by Eyre and Spottiswoode, London, in 1927. The two color halftone illustrations have been omitted from the book interior and appear on the covers. The Appendix at the end of the book is included for historical interest only.

International Standard Book Number

ISBN-13: 978-0-486-49700-6
ISBN-10: 0-486-49700-3

Manufactured in the United States by Courier Corporation
49700301 2013
www.doverpublications.com

To Absent Friends.

A SILENT TOAST TO THE
ROW OF LITTLE TOMBSTONES
IN MY GARDEN.

CONTENTS

DOGS
OF CHARACTER

MICKY CRACKER

PROLOGUE

WHICH TELLS YOU HOW TO GET A DOG

THIS book is about just ordinary dogs—dogs of character —and not necessarily about champions and prize-winners.

Although the chief characters in my medley are my own two dogs—Cracker and Micky—I shall also talk about the characteristics of many other dogs and breeds.

To Cracker and Micky I give the limelight, because I want you all to know them, and because they have the most character of my present-day collection.

In breeds, a bull terrier and an Irish wolfhound ; in disposition, " parfait gentilmen."

If you are not already a dog owner, the first thing to do is to get a dog yourself.

How does one get a dog, then ; and when one has got him, how feed, house, and train him ?

Before getting a dog, as in stockings and gloves, it is best to have some idea what sized dog you want, whether a St. Bernard, weighing 150 lb., or a toy terrier, a few ounces.

This is important and will probably depend upon many things.

First, the size of your house.

Secondly, the amount of your previous " doggy " experience.

Thirdly, the views of your parents on the subject, if you should be living at home.

And, lastly, the length of your purse.

Let us, for example, decide that you wish to become the

AN "ORDINARY ROUGH-HAIRED TERRIER"

owner of what is known as an "ordinary rough-haired terrier."

Now, there are many ways of getting such a dog, and the first and most unreliable is to hear of a friend's friend who has one he will give you.

Like a gift hound, on no account accept it.

A better way to get a rough-haired terrier is to find out

A SAINT BERNARD

A TOY TERRIER

the name of some breeder of wire-haired fox terriers—as one variety of rough-haired terrier is called in the dog world—and write, or see him at a show, when you can ask him if he has a puppy for sale not likely to make a prize-winner, but a dog with "character," suitable as a companion.

Breeders of show dogs generally have a few misfits—puppies that will never make champions or win a prize—and these can often be bought at a very reasonable figure.

I am, of course, surmising that you only want a dog as a companion, and not for show purposes.

The names of these breeders can be found in the "doggy" papers—the "Dog World" and others, and also in any show catalogue. At the end of this book will be found the names and addresses of the secretaries of the various dog clubs.

It must be understood that a "rough-haired terrier" has many distinct varieties, and although to the non-doggy mind it signifies some sort of a wire-haired fox terrier, to the show exhibitor it may mean many types.

Here are some of the rough-haired terrier breeds, with my

A SEALYHAM PUPPY

own description of them as I see them at the modern dog show.

THE SEALYHAM TERRIER.

In a show specimen he has most of his coat pulled out, with the exception of that growing on his nose and legs.

Notwithstanding this, he is a very nice little fellow at home, and looks nothing like he does when plucked for showing.

He is a sportsman, short on the leg and cloddy, with a fairly thick head and long, low body—being about 8 to 12 inches from the ground at the shoulder—in coat hard and rough; in fact, he should look the type of dog fit to go to ground for a badger.

In real life, his coat does not grow long on his nose and legs alone. Show specimens are got up for the footlights.

Sealyhams are one of the most popular breeds. In colour they are mostly white with slight marking, tan or badger-pie on head.

Another breed of rough-haired terrier is the

WEST HIGHLAND WHITE TERRIER.

He is whitey-cream in colour, short-legged and strongly

AN ABERDEEN TERRIER

built, small prick ears and an undocked tail about 6 inches long—hard coat but not curly. His job was originally to go to ground for fox or otter, so he should be a hard-looking sort.

Also there is the

SCOTCH TERRIER or ABERDEEN,

another rough-haired terrier of the short-legged, undocked type, with a hard coat, black, grey or wheaten or various shades of brindle in colour, ears small and erect, a long, punishing head and compact body.

The DANDIE DINMONT, the CAIRN, and BORDER terriers are all distinct rough-haired terrier breeds, although the last may easily be mistaken by the novice for a late inhabitant of the Battersea Dogs' Home.

Of the larger breeds of rough-haired terriers we have the

IRISH TERRIER,

whose appearance on the show bench is also very different to what

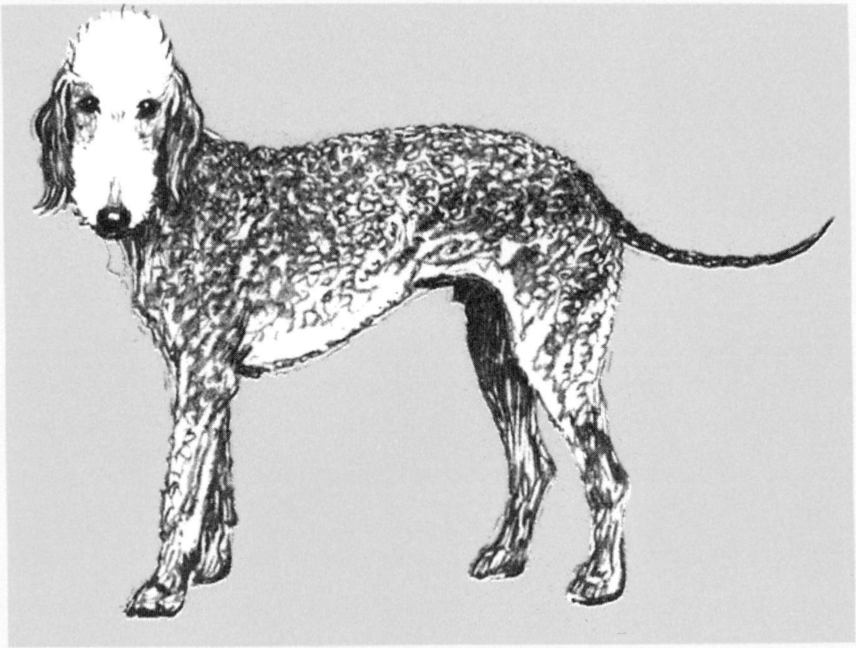

A BEDLINGTON TERRIER

it is in ordinary clothes ; and the same applies, but still more so, to the Airedale, whose show make-up, to the non-doggy visitor, has now become ludicrous.

One wonders whether a show Airedale has to have his neck shaved once or twice a day before going for exhibition.

Besides these, we have two genuinely comic customers, the BEDLINGTON and the KERRY BLUE TERRIER, the Bedlington, in his show dress, looking like a mixture of grey

A KERRY BLUE TERRIER

ferret, rat and Dandie Dinmont, and the latter a dog whose chief characteristic is a long blue or black beaver beard.

So that if you are getting a rough-haired terrier, there is a considerable number of breeds to select from.

Another way of getting a rough-haired terrier, or, for that matter, any sort of cheap canine companion, is to pay a visit to the Dogs' Home at Battersea, where you can pick out any dog you like, after they have been in the home a certain number of days awaiting their allotted span before entering the lethal chamber, for the small sum of ten shillings or one pound.

You may take home any one you fancy—but, like buying a horse at auction without a warranty or vet.'s certificate, you will be buying a conundrum.

You may get a *rough-haired* terrier-looking dog, but you may also get a mixture of a good many other breeds included.

On the other hand, character is to be found at the Dogs' Home, and a mongrel has often as much or even more of this than a show terrier, who sometimes never goes out of his range of kennels except to attend shows, and does not always have the close human companionship necessary to fully develop his character.

All the foregoing is on the assumption that you want simply a dog companion.

Having got your terrier, how do you propose to feed, house, and train him ?

Is he to be an outside dog or a house dog ?

If the former, he must have a daily run, not on the chain, and should have at least one good meal each evening with water always within reach.

His chain must be fairly long, with no possibility of getting it hung up on adjacent objects.

The best plan of all is to have a tightly pegged-down stout wire on the ground, about 12 feet or more in length, and a running chain upon this.

He should always have straw or shavings in his kennel, which should be sound and watertight, slightly raised off the ground, and big enough for him to lie down in with comfort.

However, as this book is of dogs of character, and the

AT THE DOGS' HOME, BATTERSEA

chained-up yard dog will never have his character fully developed, neither will he be the companion to his owner that his luckier indoor brother will become, his unhappy life-story does not arise!

If you have a dog at all, and want a dog of character, don't condemn him to a solitary, chained-up existence.

Dogs love human companionship—love to have and know a master or mistress—and if properly trained and exercised will always behave themselves in the house.

Many people prefer to have a puppy, training him themselves from the beginning, and this is by far the better plan.

Now, puppies, like all young things, are by nature mischievous.

They will tear up gloves, stockings, and soft shoes if the opportunity occurs, and if not corrected for doing so; but at the same time, the owner must remember that this tearing up of things is only the natural instinct of anything young.

The best age to buy a puppy is between four and six months, if possible over distemper.

At this age the dog is not too young to correct, and if purchased from a breeder's kennel has not developed any bad house habits, therefore the training of him will be your own.

The first thing to do is to give your dog a name and teach him to answer to it and come when called; to lie down when told, and to give up all ideas of chewing any of your socks, gloves and slippers.

This is not always easy with a puppy of determination, but your new youngster will probably not be much good or in proper health unless he has this characteristic.

A dog should never be allowed to get into the habit of expecting food at your own meal times, but should be taught to lie down quietly during meals; neither should he be brought into the room at all until he has learnt to obey the order to lie down.

With small dogs this is not quite so important as with the larger breeds—but with all of these latter it is imperative, for your own and your visitors' comfort, that your dog should be taught to " down " at the word of command.

The best way of all is to teach him to lie in one particular place during your meal times and to see that this place is well out of the way of the service department.

When your puppy arrives, if you wish to keep him and train him for the house, see that he is taken outside into the garden for a few minutes, at least every two hours, during the first two or three days. Trouble taken now will save a deal of annoyance later, as dogs very quickly develop a habit.

Severe correction must be given should any accident arise indoors, with immediate ejectment of the culprit to the garden.

In three days, if this plan is followed, your puppy will have learnt what is expected of him; and as you have been gradually lengthening the period of his indoor time during these three days, according to the rapidity with which his lesson is learnt, the garden period has probably developed into one morning and one afternoon walk.

You cannot train a puppy, however, without at least one licking, and, without wishing to be accused of cruelty, it must be one, if only a hand spanking, which will make him really cry

"TEACH HIM TO LIE IN ONE PARTICULAR PLACE"

out. The best instrument of chastisement is a very thin and pliable switch, correction always being given at the time of the fault and adjacent to the misdemeanour.

It is this first correction that a dog remembers. Therefore, if you wish to bring up your dog well, do not be too soft-hearted over it. It will save you a lot of trouble in the end, and the dog a lot of future hidings.

Don't think me a brute, dear ladies; for if you want to bring up your children well, you will, I am sure, realize that early and firm correction of faults is the real road to success.

The question of housing your new puppy at night is the first problem of the new dog owner. Having followed my plan, you may find on the first day that everything has worked satisfactorily—but you cannot be expected to get up every few hours through the night to walk out with the dog.

One way to treat this is to have a nice warm kennel full of straw in your garden, or on a veranda, and when you chain him up give him his first meal—a very big meal—outside this kennel.

Leave him to eat it and he will probably curl up in the straw soon afterwards. If a stable loose box is available, it is of course much better for him than being chained up at nights for the first few days—but any outside shed answers the purpose equally well.

He may, of course, howl—puppies *have* been known to do such things when first shut out at night—but if his supper is big enough (don't be frightened of over-feeding him the first night) he will soon curl up in his warm bed and go to sleep.

Don't feed him much during the day—get him really hungry if you want to sleep in comfort yourself, and then feed him at the place in which you intend him to sleep.

The warmer his bed the more likely you are to rest in peace.

In a day or two, when he has become quite accustomed to his night nursery and has learnt to connect it with his supper, he should be given a run for a few minutes after he has eaten his meal, but this need not be done until he is thoroughly used to his sleeping quarters.

Having brought you through my Prologue, procured you your dog, and given you a few words of advice as to his first treatment and housing, let me introduce you to some of my own dogs, and through them, their education and characters, endeavour to give some further hints on the bringing-up of your companion.

"HE MAY, OF COURSE, HOWL"

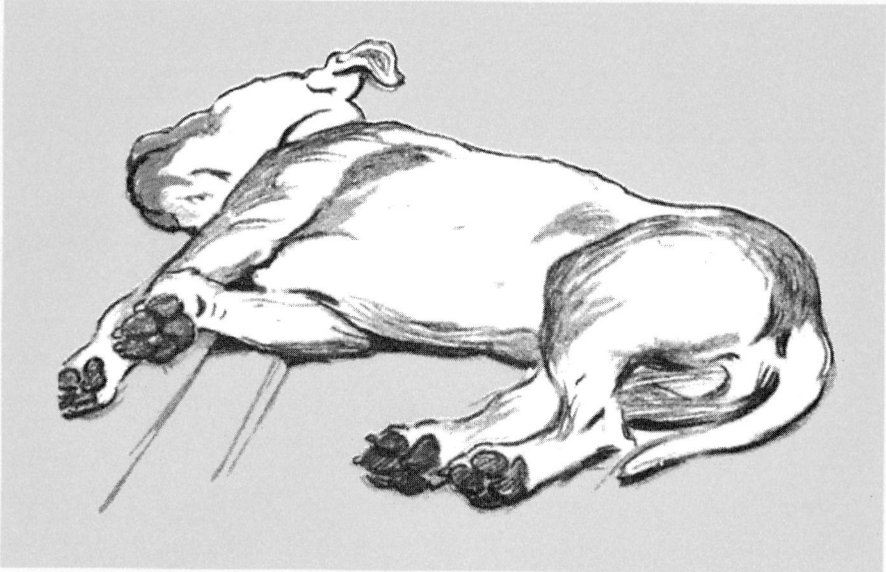

"THE WARMER HIS BED THE MORE LIKELY YOU ARE
TO REST IN PEACE"

CHAPTER I

WHICH TELLS YOU HOW TO TRAIN YOUR DOG NOW YOU HAVE GOT HIM

EVERY dog has a character of some sort—some good, some undeveloped, and some few bad.

My two dogs, Micky and Cracker, come under the first category; also they are both prize-winners at dog shows, Micky having won the prize at Salisbury for

THE MOST POPULAR DOG IN THE SHOW

(voted for by ballot by the visitors), and Cracker securing his honours at Porlock Weir by winning the prize as

THE UGLIEST DOG IN THE SHOW.

What they don't know about prize-winning isn't worth knowing, and never again shall I think that show dogs have not as much character as mongrels.

They came to me in this way.

Having tea one afternoon with a friend who breeds Irish wolfhounds (there were seven in the room with us), my wife very definitely decided that it was time for me to give her a present, and Micky, one of the three-months-old puppies, *had* to be bought.

Also with us at tea was a good-looking lady breeder of bull terriers. I fancy, seeing how easily I seemed to fall to the wolfhound suggestion, that she thought one of her dogs was also indicated, and suggested, as a stable companion for Micky, a bull terrier puppy of the same age.

This suggestion I at first declined—my kennel, or rather house, being already full of dogs.

No! I did *not* want a bull terrier.

My lady friend, however, was a very astute business woman, murmuring in my ear what pals bull terriers were, and how she had *the* most comic-looking puppy ever whelped.

I began, against my bank-balance self, to waver; partly because I am much more interested in a comic-looking dog than in a show specimen, and partly because the owner had a most persuasive manner. Added to this, her description of Cracker, his comic black spot over one eye, and his most decided character, intrigued me, got me wobbling. In the end I fell, agreeing to buy the puppy (unseen), which was to be sent to me the following week.

Racing tipsters never seem to take their own valuable advice in backing horses, and this, as I have said, is the worst way of all to buy a dog.

That's how Cracker came.

Mick and Crack, their abbreviated names (and what self-respecting dog has not got an abbreviated name?) made friends at once—a friendship which has remained, even to the extent of nightly sharing bones together, without one single grouse or grumble. They slept together, played together, and were educated together; and if Micky was away from his friend for half an hour, the fuss Cracker would make on his return, jumping round him with delight and affectionately licking his face, nose and roof of his mouth, while the wolfhound yawned with boredom, would have made a stranger imagine that these two friends had been separated for weeks.

In the days of their education food, as usual, was the stumbling

"MICK AND CRACK . . . MADE FRIENDS AT ONCE"

block upon which both of them first fell away from the straight and narrow path.

As Micky grew up, and when his head reached above the level of the dining-room table, he strolled one evening into this room while a meal was being prepared.

The maid had left a butter dish on a low dresser while she returned kitchenwards to fetch other things, and on her return found the dish completely emptied and Micky looking greasy about the chops and very stout about the middle.

He remembered his lesson, and has never been known to steal again. I gave it to him at once, directly after the crime had been committed.

If a dog is to have a hiding, give it to him immediately after the offence; then he knows and understands what it is for. To come home an hour or so afterwards and then give your dog a hiding teaches him nothing—" lots of lickings for the things he never done " not being the system to go upon.

Besides once eating butter *en masse*, Mick has other fancies in the way of food.

When in the kitchen-garden he will always go straight to the brussels sprouts bed and bite off the young tops, eating them with obvious relish; and at supper, on brussels sprouts night, when he has this green meat mixed with his food, his meal disappears almost before the others have begun.

His one other failing is strawberries. I have known a cat with a liking for asparagus, but an Irish wolfhound loving strawberries is, I think, uncommon. Luckily, in the fruit season our growing strawberries are always netted in, but at that time Mick is constantly to be found prowling round the edge of the netting, greedily biting off and eating any strawberries that have managed to push their way through the wire mesh.

The three-tier afternoon tea-cake stand is also a terrible trial to dogs when first they meet it alone in a room.

Which reminds me of a Sealyham terrier I once owned, known

to all of us as The Blighter, who was *the* most accomplished cake-stand thief I have ever come across.

With a tea-time room full of people The Blighter would lie down in a strategic position near the cake stand, with a look of angelic innocence on his face, behaving himself all the while like the most perfect little gentleman imaginable, and not attempting to "beg" or worry any of my friends for food.

No cake would ever tempt *him*—not even the lowest plate containing, as he knew full well, only bread and butter; only to the doggy C.I.D. man was he given away as a suspicious character by the copious dribble from the corners of his mouth.

"THE BLIGHTER"

Here he would lie, with his head resting on his forepaws, gazing at everybody in turn, awaiting the one auspicious moment when the buzz of chatter had reached fever heat (which it sometimes does when many ladies are gathered together), and then, with one window-snatching dive, he would make a dart at the stand, gulping as many sweet cakes into his mouth as he could cram into it. Having accomplished this, he would, almost before those in the room had discovered his theft, immediately dash for the door and outside passage, leaving a trail of broken and half-eaten cakes behind him.

Of course, he was always caught and duly, and severely, chastised, but he was never what one could call a *safe* dog with the cake stand, although he was never known to steal at any other time, neither did he attempt to steal cakes when we were alone or when two or three people, talking quietly, were in the room.

It was only when a great buzz of conversation arose, and when he was completely forgotten, that Blighter, the crook, would give his artistic exhibition of how a cake stand should be raided.

I have mentioned before that dogs should always be taught to lie down during meals, and I learnt this when staying some years ago with Lord Lonsdale at Barleythorpe.

A wonderful dog trainer, all his dogs were under the most perfect control and knew the meaning of every intonation of their master's voice.

The first night I dined there my host asked me how many dogs I thought he had in the room, and, on looking round, I could not *see* a single dog.

There were, however, eight of golden retriever and other breeds, and at a low whistle from their master they all came out from their hiding-places and stood round his chair.

Each dog had his own particular " place in the sun "—his own piece of furniture under which he remained all through the meal unless called out by Lord Lonsdale himself.

Micky was very easy to train to lie down ; but Cracker, being of a more shy disposition, had to be very carefully handled in order not to make him cowed when the order was given to " down."

One word of encouragement to Cracker will get him jumping round you with delight, but a severe tone in the voice immediately has the opposite effect and sends his tail down and his ears hanging low on each side of his broad head. But he never *wants* to do wrong as soon as he can understand what it is you want him to do. He is always looking at you, trying to discover what it is you want.

At first, Cracker would daily take up a sitting position under a small table during meals, and it was some time before he followed the other dogs' example and got right down on to the floor.

I think, like a naughty little boy, he must have got ashamed of being the only dog sitting up.

"CRACKER WOULD DAILY TAKE UP A SITTING POSITION UNDER A SMALL TABLE"

All my dog friends have a passion for weak tea. I have an idea—probably any veterinary surgeon will tell me an entirely erroneous one—that weak tea is an antidote for distemper. Anyhow, they all have it after our own tea is over, " ladies first " being the rule, each dog having a basin or saucer of tea in turn and not moving until his name is called and his own tea ready.

Although the bravest of dogs when thoroughly roused, there is no doubt bull terriers are shy as youngsters and even as older dogs. They also have a habit of eating themselves out of any strange place in which they may be shut up. Some years before Cracker came on the scene I had a full-grown dog named Sturdee, and he also was very shy.

On his first arrival he was shut up for a short time in a loose box, and in half an hour had nearly eaten himself through a solid oak door. Then he was put in my studio yard with a couple of terrier bitches (and for goodness' sake, ladies, let us call them by their proper names and not " lady dog "—we surely have passed the Victorian era), but promptly jumped a five-foot wall, and was caught with the greatest difficulty before bolting away.

I then had him in my studio all day with me and, as he seemed to have settled down, left him there when going into the house for tea.

On my return, all I found in place of my bull terrier was a large hole in the door and a heap of torn-off wood on the floor.

Making every inquiry, we could hear nothing of him that night, but early the next morning I made a circular cast in my car of the villages round, discovering that he had been seen jogging towards the main Bath Road some few miles away. As he rivalled Cracker in ugliness he was not likely to be missed by passers-by.

Then, having hit his line, I began to hear of him at different villages along the road; and after travelling, with constant stoppages for inquiries, some eight or nine miles, found a young policeman who told me that he believed his sergeant had shortly before enticed a stray bull terrier into the station, and had got him shut up.

Stopping my engine outside the police station, I heard a familiar noise of wood being torn asunder, and at once knew that I had found Sturdee.

On seeing the sergeant I was informed that there was a shilling to pay and that my dog was safely shut up in one of the cells.

" Perhaps you would like to let him out yourself, sir," said my friend. " He's an ugly-looking customer. The first door on the right down the passage—it's not locked."

Quickly paying my humble shilling, I thanked him and started off to get Sturdee, knowing quite well in my own mind that my bull terrier would by this time be well on his way to freeing himself, and that another five minutes' wait might have saved me the payment.

On turning into the passage I had no difficulty in finding the door, as his pink nose was already protruding through a large hole which he had succeeded in making in the woodwork—and through which he was about to make his own exit.

This habit of biting a way out must be a characteristic of the

" STURDEE "

bull terrier breed, as both my bull terriers—although in no way related—have at once attempted to do this whenever shut up in unknown surroundings.

Any dog might try to do it as a last resource if shut up in a room for some time.

A Scotch terrier of mine had this trait developed in a peculiar way, but she would only tear up everything she could get her teeth into in the room.

Shut up once by mistake in a bedroom and forgotten for the greater part of a day, she completely demolished two pillow cases, all the cushions, the seats of two chairs and the bed valances—even biting the wallpaper from the lower part of the walls and tearing parts of the carpet to shreds.

She must have seen red, and given way to hysterical rage, because on no other occasion was she ever destructive nor had she ever been known to tear up anything.

Now Mick and Cracker were always the best of friends; as they played, so they dined and slept—always together—but as their daily routine, even as regards games, hardly ever varies, may I give it to you?

At 9 o'clock they leave their bedroom and are taken for a short walk in the fields.

9.30, light breakfast—dog biscuit, vimlets and hound-meal.

10.30 to 11.30, walking exercise with horses three days a week.

11.30 to 1, at work in the studio.

1 to 2, see their master eat his luncheon and walk round the garden afterwards.

2 to 4.15, at work in the studio.

4.15 to 4.30, walk out with groom.

4.40, half a bowl of weak tea, sugar and milk.

5 to 7, at work in studio.

7, supper and walk out afterwards in garden and paddock.

8 to 10, sleep in the house.

10 o'clock, stable; and so to bed.

That, roughly, is their routine, but arising from this are many things which help to show their character.

Cracker is always the clown of the party, and as the clown he has certain daily jokes to play off upon the other dogs. Of these jokes, each of which has its definite fixed time in Cracker's day, the first occurs at 9.2 when Jane, the Airedale terrier, and Bogie, the er—er—, just rough-haired terrier, join the company.

For the first hundred yards of the walk Cracker charges his 60 lb. against Jane, who is the old maid of the party, taking no notice of her protests and attempts to "keep herself to herself."

The effect is the same as when a small man is charged by a heavy one at football—Jane being sent sprawling every time.

At 9.7, when all the dogs are in the meadow, as soon as my man or myself turns for home Cracker lags behind for his daily morning romp with Mick.

Here he waits until the others are a hundred yards away, when he charges after them, making as he comes zigzagging swerves in every direction, pretending to be a mad dog. When he has covered half the distance, Mick—who has been lying in the

"THEIR MORNING ROUGH-AND-TUMBLE"

grass watching him—now cuts him off, and Cracker in his turn is rolled over and over as they have their morning rough-and-tumble.

This same game takes place at 4.15.

But, after supper, another joke is always brought off by the clown—which is played with one particular dog with whom he plays at no other time during the day.

In the winter months their after-supper walk takes place in the dark in the garden, and whoever takes them out carries a stable lantern.

Very soon after arriving in the garden Cracker will hide in the dark yew and laurel bushes which surround my lawn, suddenly making a spook-like dash out from some unexpected spot, not at Jane, but at Bogie.

Now Bogie is a quiet, harmless, and sedate little thing, walking on her own and not playing with anyone, but she knows perfectly well each night that Cracker will pounce out from some dark bush upon her, and for that reason keeps close to the lighted lantern, peering anxiously into every dark place or bush until her martyrdom commences and Cracker gives her her nightly shock. After being pounced upon by the bull terrier she is

"FIRMLY TAKEN BY THE COLLAR AND DRAGGED ON HER BACK ROUND THE LAWN"

"CRACKER THRUSTING HIS 60 LB. WEIGHT ON THE TOP OF HIM"

firmly taken by the collar by him and dragged on her back round the lawn, until her shrieks for help become too heartrending and she is finally rescued by Mick.

As in the daytime, so in the house after supper a regular routine is followed—Micky always taking up a position on his own couch and Cracker thrusting his 60 lb. weight on the top of him. No groans from Mick will stop the bull terrier from making himself quite comfortable, as a rule getting his red nose well tucked away into Mick's now soft and well-filled middle.

"QUITE COMFORTABLE"

At supper time they have learnt, with my other dogs, to wait until their names are called when their evening meal is ready, in the same way that hounds are "drawn" to feed.

Each dog's dish is placed in a separate part of the stable which adjoins the house, and they then line up inside. When the doors are open the name of each dog is called separately, and he dashes across the yard to his own supper dish—never, on pain of dire punishment, touching any of the other dogs' food. No dog is allowed to go until his name is called, and, as they never know whose name will be called first, excitement is always intense.

Here again Cracker was more difficult to train than Micky and the others; and during the earlier lessons, if his name was not called first, I know he thought seriously of charging me over and taking the consequences.

Now, however, on these occasions he is a perfect little gentleman, if a very excited one.

This hound system of drawing by name to feed enforces obedience to its fullest extent, and is a very excellent training for all dogs. Care, however, should be taken that when they have finished their own food they should not be allowed to join issue with others who have not done so: my pack only being allowed to go to the other dishes when an order is given and all are ready to change over.

Bones should never be given at this time—but each dog may have one bone afterwards if given in a separate run.

With regard to food. Each dish is, of course, mixed separately according to the size and necessity of the dog in question.

Fish, chicken, or game bones should never be given to dogs, but any large bones are good for them even if containing very little meat.

With such friends as my two principals, the rule as to giving bones separately is broken. Bone time with them is after their evening walk, and each has one big bone given to him to chew for half an hour in a stone-flagged passage in the house.

SUPPER TIME

"NO DOG IS ALLOWED TO GO UNTIL HIS NAME IS CALLED"

Now, although Micky stands 36 inches at the shoulder and Cracker only 19, the latter can in time chew up any sized bone, while Mick very soon has to give his up as a bad job.

When Mick has gone as far as he can with his own bone he will lie down by Cracker's side waiting to pick any small pieces that the bull terrier may scrunch off; Cracker afterwards helping Mick to demolish his own discarded bone.

A dog of character will often develop little habits and tricks, but I never knew any dog who kept so definitely to routine in these tricks as Cracker. At any time of the day one knows exactly what games he will be playing and with whom he will be playing them.

At 4 o'clock, to the minute, he finishes his sleep in front of my fire and will walk up to me and quietly—very quietly—catch hold of the loose part of my trouser-leg and give gentle little pulls at it. If I take no notice of this he will fetch my whip, or hat, if they are in the room, and lay them at my feet as a suggestion—only a suggestion, of course—that at 4.15 we go out for a short walk.

Then, if I place my hat on my head, even without rising from the chair in which I am sitting, every dog is immediately on his feet, and Cracker will bound round me with delight—so pleased to see that at last my sluggish brain has been able to understand his meaning.

"EVERY DOG IS IMMEDIATELY ON HIS FEET"

"HE WILL FETCH MY WHIP, OR HAT"

A BRITISH BULLDOG

CHAPTER II

WHICH TELLS OF TATTERS AND SOME OTHERS

TATTERS was a wired-haired fox terrier and had more character than any dog I have ever owned.

"WE THOUGHT WE WERE TO HAVE THE LIMELIGHT"

He came to me when about eighteen months old and was given to me by a friend's friend, the one way I advise you not to get a dog.

The exception, however, proves the rule, and notwithstanding his previous history, which was that he had developed a

Although the author will take every reasonable care that interruptions from Micky and Cracker shall not occur, he cannot hold himself responsible for interference with his narrative in parts which to the two principal characters may appear uninteresting or detracting from themselves as leading characters.

doubtful temper, he stayed with me as my constant friend and companion until his death many years afterwards.

Now, Tatters was like a dog-hound—he did not care to be mauled about—and he was very decided about it.

Tatters was a man's man.

He was not bad-tempered—in fact, I found him just the opposite—but he did *not* want to be "fussed about," owing to his chief characteristic—his independence.

Tatters walked on his "lone."

He loved a scrap—an open-air life, and in a crowd he was in his element.

When we first owned Tatters we lived at Henley, and Henley Regatta week was his great week of the year. Hardly at home a moment of the four days, he was the busiest official on the course. With every crew he went down the towing-path to Temple Island for the start, and returned as the race was run, barking his loudest as he dashed back along the bank to the winning post with the rival boats and their supporters.

My children, in a punt on the water, would eagerly look for Tatters as every race came down the course.

At the end of the four days he was so tired out that he generally slept for a whole day, but he had had his one glorious week of the year.

Once, when the Royal Agricultural Show came to Henley, we missed Tatters; but on going to the Show in the afternoon there was our friend (although "No Dogs Admitted" was plentifully posted up at the turnstiles) busily superintending events in the horse ring, immediately dodging among the crowd when any official tried to catch him.

Needless to say we cut him dead; he just wagged his stump as he recognized us, but had no time to stay with us as he was a great deal too busy.

But Tatters had many sides to his character; one thing he abhorred, and that was a bath.

"ONE THING HE ABHORRED, AND THAT WAS A BATH"

Occasionally he had to go through with it, being washed by my wife in the scullery sink.

I have heard some bad dog language in my time, but Tatters, during these bathing operations, had the most wonderful flow of language of any dog I have known. A stranger standing outside would have thought that my wife, or whoever was with the dog, was being torn to pieces.

I think his previous owners must have tried to give him a bath, hence the character for bad temper with which he came to us.

Although Tatters' oaths flew the whole time of the operation—in fact, from the time he saw my wife in an overall—he never once attempted to bite.

This was probably due to the fact that his language was absolutely ignored, just in the way a good nurse would wash a naughty little boy who objected.

At the beginning of the Great War many Engineer units

were sent to my home on the river for pontoon training, each unit being in the village for a week or a fortnight, and then moving off for another company to take their place.

Tatters treated every single officer and man in khaki as his master; and attached himself to each unit as soon as it arrived, generally taking possession of the officers' mess.

Rebuffs were useless with him; he just walked out at one door growling and walked in again, wagging his tail, at the next entrance, or the next time the door was opened.

About once every two or three days he would return home; trotting into the house wagging his tail to give everyone a "Cheerio!" and then dash off again to look after his unit.

On two or three occasions he marched to Aldershot with the outgoing company, but as his name and address were on his collar the mess generally sent me a line to say that he had come away with them. In the end I had a collar made with a request on it not to take him away from the village—"Sergeant Tatters. Please do not take me away"—and I am glad to say notice was generally sent me when the unit was leaving, when he had to be chained up for a day.

Tatters, however, did not attach himself to individuals in khaki—it was the whole mess or the whole regiment that was *his* for the time being, and any officer in uniform, whether stranger or otherwise, was always sure of an enthusiastic welcome from him.

In a town or elsewhere during the war the sight of anyone in khaki would immediately set his tail and hindquarters wagging, with a "pleased-to-meet-you" wriggle of his body. Tatters spent his days welcoming every khaki-clad soldier he met. There never was such a busy dog during the first few months of the war.

Another thing he loved was a car—but I think this is usual with most dogs. Tatters, however, did not mind whose, and the greatest care had to be taken that he did not disappear in the back of a stranger's car when stopping at a garage.

As long as his own car was available he would use that, but woe betide the stranger who tried to open the door if he was left in charge.

I remember out hunting once sending a second horseman back to my car for something after the day's sport had started. Tatters, left in charge, would have none of it, although he knew the man perfectly well, and they were the greatest friends at home; finally my messenger had to return to me without carrying out my instructions.

Tatters was also a self-feeder, but he was never a thief.

At one time I was constantly away motoring, for a week or more at a time, journeying and staying a night or two in towns and villages all over England, and taking Tatters with me as my only companion. The procedure was this, I slept in the nearest hotel and Tatters slept in the car in the hotel garage. On arrival my friend would leave me and stroll off to view the town—quite self-possessed and quite at home—as if he had lived in it all his life. But first of all he sniffed out a

"AND STROLL OFF TO VIEW THE TOWN"

pastrycook, or restaurant of some sort, and his method of procuring a meal I discovered on one or two occasions by following him at a distance.

First of all, he always chose the busiest and "shoppiest" part of the town. As soon as he winded a pastrycook or similar shop, he would coolly push the door open with his nose, if it were possible to do so, and walk in wagging his tail—there was no doubt about Tatters' tail wagging when he did it. Failing the door opening with the nose operation, he would squeeze in behind some customer.

Once safely inside he would sit up and beg, waving his paws in the air, solemnly doing this in the centre of the shop, until some kind-hearted assistant or customer threw him something.

This operation he would continue doing until he was ejected growling, or had had enough.

In the latter case his method of exit was simple. Walking to the door he would give a short, sharp bark, and if this failed to bring one of the assistants to open it for him—they were generally convulsed with laughter by this time at his independence—he continued to give these barks at short intervals until someone *did* let him out.

There was never any doubt about what Tatters wanted.

Once outside he would go back to the garage, jump into his car—the door of which was always left unlatched for him—and sleep, continuing the same feeding operation whenever he felt hungry again.

There was only one great fear Tatters had, and that was that his car would start away without him.

If he were not in sight in the morning I only had to give a loud hoot on my horn (he always knew my car's hoot from any other), and if within hearing he would immediately streak for the car as hard as he could lay feet to the ground—if you have ever seen a greyhound racing after an electric hare it will give you an idea of how he came to the sound of my

" HE WOULD IMMEDIATELY STREAK FOR THE CAR "

horn. If not within hearing, I went slowly down the High Street, touching my horn occasionally, and invariably Tatters would appear from some food emporium, or I would hear his insistent bark behind some closed door.

Horses and cars were his especial favourites; dogs he did not care so much about.

When I first had him I had a small two-seater car, and in one of his early rides, as the car was slowly passing another dog, Tatters decided to jump out and investigate. Now, jumping from a car, even when it is going very slowly, gives one a nasty jar, and Tatters nearly broke his back. Even in this, however, his character came to the top, for instead of yelling and screaming as any other dog would have done, he picked himself up and limped growling and cursing back towards the house from which I had only just started.

He never jumped or attempted to jump out of a car again, although he would sometimes ride alone in the dicky behind. No other dog, however pugnacious-looking, could ever lure him from his perch if the car was in motion.

In the course of years Tatters went completely blind, but even then, whenever he could get out of the house unseen, he would take his lone walks.

At that time I went to live at Hunt Kennels, my drive joining a busy main road.

It was on a very dangerous curve for motor traffic, and we had many dog tragedies during our first few years.

Tatters, however, although he was blind in one eye when we went there, and completely blind in both after two or three months, did not meet his end in this way, although the anxiety to his owners was acute.

All through his life he had been quite able to look after himself, and now that he was blind he did the same.

Daily he would take his lone walk to the village, to get to which he had to cross the main road at this dangerous corner opposite my house, the only footpath being on the opposite side to my entrance.

He would smell his way to the drive gate, and then always wait for some seconds listening before going straight across this road.

If a car could be heard at all—and it was either his sense of hearing or the smell of a car which warned him—he would not take a step away from the gatepost until he knew that all was clear.

Then he would feel his way straight across the tarmac road to the footpath opposite. Here he would walk along close to the wall for a hundred yards until he came to the turning to the village, where he left the tarmac main road and all was safe; the same procedure being followed on his return journey.

Always, when a car passed him, he would crouch against the wall or fence.

After a sequence of other motor dog tragedies the anxiety in the end was too great for his master, and Tatters, at a ripe old age, was peacefully laid to rest in my garden.

Requiescat in pace!

He lies in the most honoured grave in my canine cemetery.

I once had a lesson in connection with chaining up a dog which had a very sad result for my companion—a lesson which has never been forgotten.

One wet day, coming in from a walk with my dogs, I chained them up to clean before coming into the house.

Among my then collection was a big brindle bulldog, and as no other tying-up place was available, I put him on a truss of hay. Unfortunately, I did not leave him quite enough chain to reach the ground should he attempt to jump down.

What happened afterwards I can only surmise, but when I came out some little time later the bulldog was hanging with a broken neck, his hind feet only two inches from the ground.

In chaining up a dog on any raised platform it is always advisable to see that the chain is either too short to allow him to get over the edge, or long enough to allow him to stand on the ground should he wish to do so.

About this time a somewhat humorous incident happened in the same kennel.

I had been over to Belgium, and had purchased in the rag and dog market at Bruges a very large and beautifully clipped white French poodle.

Why I bought this dog I have never yet been able to

"A BEAUTIFULLY CLIPPED WHITE FRENCH POODLE"

discover, as I have never had a weakness for poodles. Youth, however, often does foolish things. Anyhow, this comic-looking dog came back to England with me.

Arriving home late in the evening, before going into the house I took my new purchase out to the terrier run, where I had some half-dozen rough-haired terriers. These terriers were always shut in the sleeping compartment at night, and as they were not to be seen in the run I at once thought that they had been shut up and slipped my poodle into it. Shutting the iron gate behind him, I hurriedly dashed into the house to greet my parents, and prepare them for the worst—my new purchase.

Before I could find them, however, I was horrified to hear from the kennel screams and yells of the most blood-curdling dog-fighting description.

The door between the run and the sleeping part had not been properly latched. Round and round the run went my white poodle, looking like a ghost in the darkness, with six yapping and snarling terriers trying to tear him to pieces.

Rushing back to his rescue I raved and stormed at them, but with no result, for as fast as I pulled one off him another fastened his teeth in the poodle's wool.

In the end, to save his life, I had to fling my terriers, one by one, over the wire railing into the garden outside.

When my family came out, hearing the commotion, they found a very muddy and bloody youth with a damaged and dishevelled poodle sitting in the dog-run, while six furious terriers raged at the railings outside.

In a previous chapter I have given some suggestions as to the way to get a dog, but if you live in the country it is always possible to " walk " a couple of foxhound puppies.

The way to get these is to write or see the huntsman at the nearest foxhound kennels, telling him that you would like to " walk " a couple of puppies for him.

It is best to advise him of this not later than March.

Now, foxhound whelps are not house dogs, and should never be brought into the house, but they want very little attention, with the exception of plenty of food and running loose all day long, with just a warm shed or stable in which they can be shut up at night.

A foxhound is not a lap-dog; he has to learn from his earliest youth how to look after himself—for that reason the huntsman prefers that his hounds should not be coddled, and wants them as youngsters to have all the exercise and freedom they can get.

Foxhound puppies are generally sent out to their "walks" at eight to ten weeks old.

Puppies of any breed, if always kept shut up, will never thrive, but with any hound breed they should be turned loose most of the day after being a few days in their new home.

A FOXHOUND PUPPY

If you "walk" a puppy for the hunt you get an invitation to the puppy show in the summer, and your puppy will compete for the prizes at this show the following year.

A "walked" puppy is sent out about March, April, or May, and can be returned to the kennels in about a year's time, when you can have another couple if you wish to do so.

His food should consist of table scraps—bones, but not chicken, fish, or game bones—with plenty of skimmed milk if available.

When he first comes he should be fed little and often, but after he is three or four months old one good meal a day will be enough, and if he gets any scraps thrown to him from the kitchen door he will do all the better.

For any illness or accident ring up the huntsman.

I once "walked" a couple of rough-haired otter-hound puppies and had a lot of fun with them hunting many things.

Every day at 5.15 the pack of one couple of otter hounds and numerous couples of basset pups would be taken by my family out into the road to pick up the line of an old farm hand who passed my house daily on the way to his cottage in the village a mile away.

"Tow-row-row-row" would go the puppies, heads down and tails up, and off would go my children behind them on hobby horses, or any kind of toy mount.

You never heard such music as the deep note of this pack, augmented by the hunting cries and horn-blowing of the riders.

Full cry each day they would carry the line to old Tom's cottage door, and after duly marking their quarry to ground the hunt would return in triumph to kennel.

Then, sometimes, they would pick up the line of a hare or moorhen (otter-hounds *have* been known to hunt a moorhen even in the hunting season), and another hunt would come off before they turned their heads for home.

Your children can get a lot of fun if you "walk" a couple of puppies.

Your gardener, probably, will not be enthusiastic, but then gardeners are generally dour Scotchmen.

Another game we used to have was with a bloodhound and an old basset-hound, Hectopotamus, of whom I shall tell you more later.

This game was known as "Hunting the Criminal"—"Bunny," that is myself, always taking the part of the quarry.

A party of children would be invited, and I need hardly tell you that everybody eagerly accepted, for the opportunity of participating in a real "man-hunt" was much too thrilling to be neglected. I enjoyed it as much as the children and, incidentally, the exercise kept me in good condition.

The criminal, having perpetrated some imaginary, dastardly deed, was allowed to escape from his prison into the pine-woods surrounding my house.

After a quarter of an hour Hectopotamus and Buster Brown, the basset and bloodhound, were laid on the line and the hunt commenced.

"HUNTING THE CRIMINAL"

Now, Potamus (his abbreviated name) had a habit of giving tongue from the moment he was laid on the line until he finally got the criminal " treed " and stood baying beneath him.

This, I am afraid, he did whether he was on the line or not, and was probably the reason that, being a good-looking basset-hound but a stray dog when I found him, no one could ever be found to claim him.

Notwithstanding this, his music helped matters with the children's hunt, the bloodhound always doing the serious work, notifying to the field in deep bays when he was on the line of his quarry.

To the villagers I was always expected to be torn to pieces when caught, but to the field of children a man-hunt was great fun, especially when Hectopotamus played a continuous orchestra until I was " eaten."

At last he had found an audience who appreciated his music.

But I must tell you how " Potamus " came to me, and of his appetite after he arrived.

A thin, stray basset-hound once came to the Hunt kennels, and as no owner could be found for him, he was given to me, as M.F.H.s do not always admire the beautiful leg curves of the common or garden basset-hound.

He was first christened " Hector " by my children, but later, as he rapidly increased in avoirdupois, " Hippopotamus " was added to it.

" HECTORHIPPOPOTAMUS,"

however, was rather a mouthful to say quickly, so we gave him a kennel name, combining the two of

" HECTOPOTAMUS,"

and at a subsequent date abbreviated it to plain

" POTAMUS."

"THE LEAN DAYS"

Hectorhippopotamus (it takes such a long time to write that we will call him " Potamus " in future) had a most abnormal appetite, possibly on account of the lean days of his straydom period, for he certainly never meant to have an empty tummy again, and of this appetite and how it saved his life I will tell you.

"RAPIDLY INCREASED IN AVOIRDUPOIS"

Now, the woman who has agreed to share for life all my doggy and other troubles would take a collection of the dogs with her when walking to the village, including the hefty Potamus.

These morning trips were the joy of the once thin basset.

Slowly he would plop, plop, plop, plop behind her, gradually "filling" up from every cottage rubbish heap, and from the outsides of the butchers', fishmongers', and bakers' shops, his keen nose never missing the minutest crumb in the way of food.

At the end of an hour's "shopping" Potamus's larder would be well filled and he would be ready to start to waddle home again.

One hot day, when he had been more than lucky in flotsam and jetsam and, in consequence, was feeling rather sluggish, a car came slowly chugging its way up the hill behind him.

My wife called to him to get out of the way, and the chauffeur, seeing the dog, slowed his car down to walking pace.

Meanwhile, Potamus went on, still keeping in the centre of the road, day-dreaming, no doubt, of the supper to come to him in the evening.

Hoot—hoot—hoot—hoot—hoot went the motor-horn, and our friend took a slow step to the side, but not quite quick enough to miss the near front wheel. Then came a shriek from my wife as the basset collapsed under the wheel itself.

The car had just enough "way," or enough horse-power, to rise partly the big mound of the tightly-packed middle of Potamus, climb to the top, then, "konking out," slowly trickled back again on to the road.

Rushing to the spot, my wife expected to pick up the corpse of the once bonny basset hound, but no more serious damage was done than a bent back rib.

My family ever afterwards put this down to the tightness of the packing in his tummy—which tightness had obviously stopped him from being killed and the car from completely surmounting so steep an incline. It was always afterwards an excuse for the children to give him some more to eat in case he was run over by another car.

While I have been writing the last few pages of this chapter, I have been feeling a gentle pull every now and then at the loose part of my trouser leg—where my bull terrier reclines at my feet.

" As you mildly suggest Cracker by trouser pulling, you two might be taking a chorus lady's part in my book, instead of the lead, for all the limelight you are getting.

" Never mind, we will finish the chapter with the story of the great day when you won your

PRIZE,

and you shall take the centre of the stage once more."

DOGS OF BREEDING

Now, both Micky and Cracker, besides being dogs of character, are also dogs of breeding.

Both of them have champions in their pedigrees, both own mothers who were champions ! ! !

Micky covered himself with glory at a Show in the South of England, where he had been entered for three classes in Irish wolfhounds, by winning the first prize in each class.*

(When the applause has subsided, Micky will resume his place on the couch.)

On the same occasion he also won the prize mentioned in Chapter I, a complete guarantee of his friendliness and amiability.

Cracker has only been shown on one occasion, but on that day he swept the boards—in his class—by winning the first prize for THE UGLIEST DOG IN THE SHOW, which proves that, in showing dogs, breeding will always win in the end.

Last summer Cracker's master was asked to get up an entertainment for a charitable purpose at Porlock Weir, and for some days neither of them could think of any novel way of worrying money out of visitors.

One day, however, CRACKER had an inspiration.

Why not a MONGREL DOG SHOW?

Then, for some hours, CRACKER and the man put their heads together, got out the following programme, and had it printed and posted all over the Devon and Somerset country:

PROGRAMME OF THE MONGREL DOG SHOW

CLASS I.—The worst mongrel.
" II.—The bandiest-legged dog.
" III.—The dog with the longest tail.
" IV.—The tail with the longest dog.
" V.—The dog with the most spots.
" VI.—The dog with the most sympathetic eyes.
" VII.—The fattest dog.
" VIII.—The ugliest dog.
" IX.—The prettiest puppy (under one year).
" X.—The biggest dog.

And so on.

* Note by Editor.—You have forgotten to mention that the other three entries in each class arrived too late to be judged.

"TOLD ALL THE DOGS ABOUT HIS IDEA"

Having done this, the master had a fit of depression, feeling that no one would acknowledge possessing a dog without champions in its pedigree, and therefore no entries would be forthcoming.

CRACKER, on the other hand, had fits of jubilation, and straightway told all the dogs in front of the Anchor Hotel about his idea.

This, in itself, takes some doing, as there are more dogs in front of the Anchor Hotel at Porlock Weir, during the summer months, than any other hotel in England.

CRACKER got the entries.

CRACKER ran the Show.

(He also will resume his seat on the couch when the applause has subsided.)

Before breakfast, on the morning of the day, Cracker and his collaborator went for a ride through Ashley Coombe Woods.

Now, a ride through the woods with Cracker is an "occasion" which, to a horse and his rider, is rather a nerve-racking entertainment, for the bull-terrier has no fear of his equine friend, and thinks nothing of doing a double somersault between the horse's hind and front legs; at any rate, that is what it seems like to the man on the horse's back.

On this morning Cracker was in better (or worse) form than ever—three times he disappeared at full gallop over what seemed the edge of the cliff, zigzagging in front of some imaginary friend chasing him.

"TWICE HE USED MY HORSE'S LEGS AS CROQUET HOOPS"

THE MONGREL DOG SHOW
JUDGING THE BANDIEST-LEGGED DOG

Twice he used my horse's legs as croquet hoops and spent the rest of the time doing somersaults, and spinning round on the end of his tail. All of which was to tell me that his Show would be a success, but which put his master's nerves into a further state of jazz.

The doors of the Show were to open at two o'clock.

About eleven o'clock Cracker and his assistant walked into Ashley Coombe to make some final arrangements, and, behold! the impresario's friends had begun to arrive.

Alsatians, bloodhounds, collies, terriers, spaniels—every known and unknown breed of dog, the only breed not attending being Corgi dogs.

" Mongrel puppy, whelp and hound, and curs of low degree."

THE MONGREL DOG SHOW
AN ENTRY IN CLASS VI: "THE DOG WITH THE MOST SYMPATHETIC EYES"

Then the smile-that-won't-come-off settled on the faces of both of the organizers.

When the Show opened, my partner, in the exuberance of his spirits, entered himself for every class, including the prettiest puppy.

In the class for "the dog with the most spots" he was disqualified by the judges, Mrs. Philip Hunloke and an ex-M.F.H., when it was discovered that his spots came off (in the hurry his dresser must have used watercolour instead of the oil-paint I had left out), narrowly escaping being hauled up before the Council of the Kennel Club for malpractices and faking.

"SOME VERY KEEN COMPETITION"

Finally, he won his only prize, as "the ugliest dog" in the Show, which he thoroughly deserved, as there was some very keen competition.

The judges only made one serious mistake, and that was in nearly giving a champion border terrier the prize for the biggest mongrel, Mrs. A. J. Munnings winning this in the end with three of the worst mongrels I have ever seen.

As these three, known far and wide as "THE BING BOYS," were completely devoid of any family likeness, either in shape, coat, colour, size, or anything else, Cracker and myself, in the interest of the morals of the other dogs exhibited, were glad that the R.A.'s wife did not exhibit the mother as well.

That was Cracker's great day last summer; I am sorry to have had to bore you with a description of it, but I promised him his "little bit of fat" to finish this chapter, and unless you wish your child to lose confidence in you, you must never promise anything you do not fulfil.

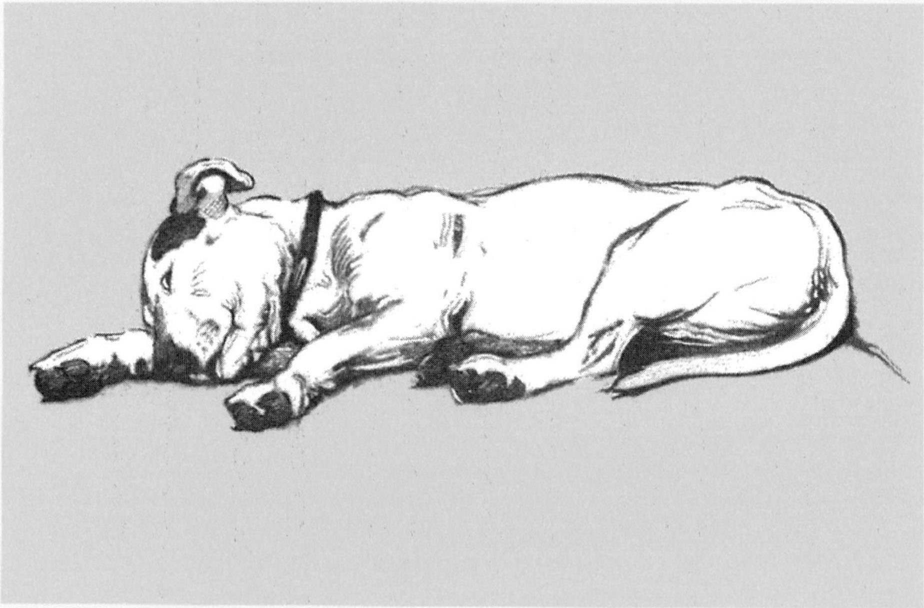

"THE END OF A PERFECT DAY"

CHAPTER III

WHICH TELLS LITTLE ABOUT DOGS, BUT A LOT ABOUT ARTISTS' MODELS

MANY years ago I had a small mongrel fox terrier who was a most accomplished professional model. She would sit without moving a muscle for twenty minutes or more, and keep immovable in any position in which she was placed.

On one occasion, when I was illustrating an article on performing dogs, I had to depict a dog standing on its head. Gyp, my model, took the pose wonderfully, and by putting her in an arm-chair with her hind legs high up the back and her head on the seat the exact position was secured.

I have some of the sketches made from her twenty-five or more years ago. She was no beauty, but she certainly had affection and character.

At that time many other dogs came to me as sitters, and her jealousy was very amusing when they were at work posing. No dog in my studio was ever allowed to go on to the model throne without being accompanied by Gyp, my professional model. This she did entirely of her own accord, solemnly walking up and sitting herself down by the side of the chained-up dog, and never moving until the other was unchained.

She had an uncanny aptitude for posing, and seemed to realize at once what was required from her when sitting. It seemed almost like hypnotism the way in which she would keep a leg out in an awkward position, never moving it until she was told to do so. I have had many other semi-professional animal models, but never such an accomplished one as my first.

A greedy dog is always a good sitter, but there are other ways for the artist to catch expression in dogs besides showing him food.

From my present studio my dogs can hear my groom as he crosses from the harness room to the stable, and immediately recognize the sound of the jingle of the bits in the bridles. Then they are all excitement to go out, and know that a walk with the horses is indicated, and by watching at my window can see all that goes on. While saddling operations are in progress their excitement reaches fever heat, and expression can then be got which even the offer of food would not secure.

That little extra raising of the eyebrow lump in a dog, the dilation of the eye, together with the wrinkles caused by the pushing forward of the ears, give that intense excitement feeling we all want to secure when painting an animal.

A smooth-coated St. Bernard once gave me a good deal of trouble as a sitter, for when once he saw me in front of my easel nothing would interest him.

Immediately this happened he would curl up on the ground and hide his head, or as much of it as he could, between his thigh and his side.

I tried him with food, liver, and showing him other dogs, but nothing would keep him awake when once he saw me prepare to paint; the sight of a pencil or paint-brush in my hand being enough to make him immediately tuck away his head and drop off to sleep.

After almost giving up I found that he would listen for the footsteps of the dogboy when out of sight, although he would take no further notice of him, if he came into view, while my sketch-book or easel were in evidence.

"GYP," AN ACCOMPLISHED MODEL

"SHE HAD AN UNCANNY APTITUDE FOR POSING, AND SEEMED TO REALIZE AT ONCE WHAT WAS REQUIRED OF HER WHEN SITTING"

"NOTHING WOULD INTEREST HIM"

By getting this boy to conceal himself in a shrubbery near by and walk up and down just out of view but within hearing, I was able to get my St. Bernard interested and keep him awake.

The boy walked many miles in a small circle that afternoon, but whenever his footsteps came within hearing distance my model woke up and took interest.

You cannot ask an animal to keep his head in one position; you have to catch him with cunning, and the difficulty that very few dogs like being looked at for long is always a trial for the animal-painter.

Cracker invariably hides his nose somewhere (it's so very red, poor dear, I think he is really rather ashamed of it), and always has to be sketched by cunning and subterfuge.

I once kept an old hunter many months simply as a model,

"DON'T FORGET THIS IS A BOOK ON DOGS"

and he became almost as clever at the job as Gyp, my terrier. These two were the best models I ever owned.

It is not easy to make detail studies of horses' legs in galloping and jumping positions—but this old warrior was a wonder for keeping his legs still in any position—provided we gave him support for them.

Many and various were the tubs and boxes arranged at different heights upon which his ancient legs have rested, stuck out in positions one could hardly believe a horse would be able to "hold."

All he wanted was a feed of oats, and we could always prop one of his four legs up on something, and he would not trouble to move it for quite a long time.

As long as he kept still he was allowed to feed, but as soon as the leg was moved the sieve was taken away. In the end, I fancy his brain must have connected any movement with indicating that his feed would disappear.

One night in Verrey's, the rendezvous of all "doggy" Bohemians in the late George R. Krehl's time, George R. Sims ("Dagonet" of the "Referee") offered to lend me as a model, a Dalmatian, of which breed he always had a considerable number. On the appointed day, just as my wife and I were sitting down to breakfast, a smart dogcart pulled up at my gate. On my front door being opened, seven panting Dalmatians plunged into the house, knocking over the maid, and in mass formation wildly rushing upstairs and into every room.

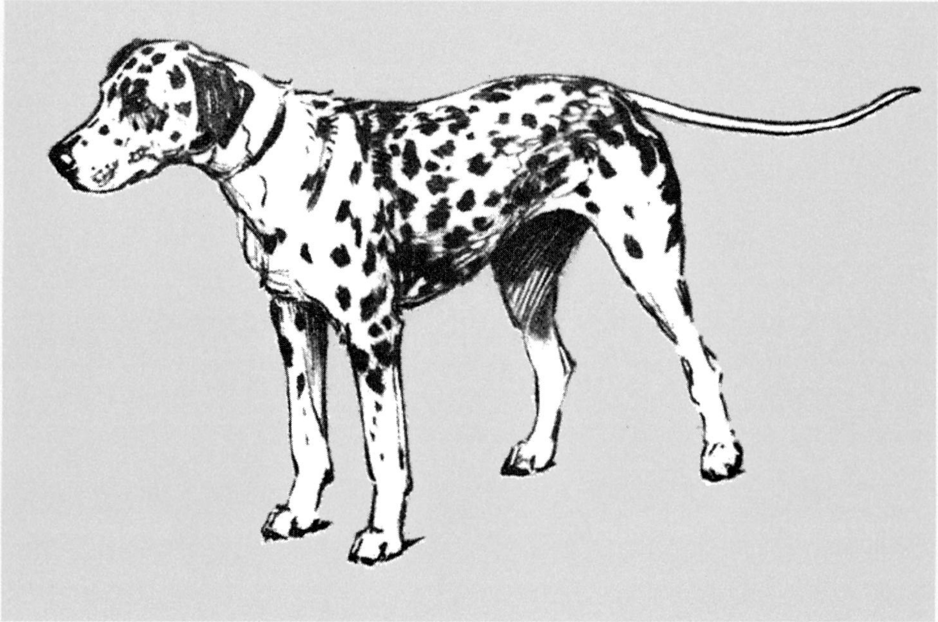

A DALMATIAN

All were delighted to see everybody, and, as seven whip tails wagged energetically round the rooms, crash, crash went many ornaments and oddments.

"Dagonet," it appeared, had sent *seven* Dalmatians for me to choose from. The man could not leave his pony, and a passing errand-boy had rung the bell; as the door opened in had rushed, pleased as Punch, this pack of plum puddings.

A little disconcerting to have seven large, strange and spotted plum-pudding dogs mixed up with your breakfast—a time when we arc not always feeling our brightest and best.

The first foxhound I ever owned was when I was living at Chiswick. He came from the Essex Union as a model, an old hound which had been given to me by the Master for this purpose—I was certainly very young at the time to have attempted to keep a foxhound in London.

Under my studio I had a stable, and into a loose box on his first arrival, Furrier, for that was his name, was duly installed.

Among my other pets at that time was a West African monkey, who also had her bedroom in a cage in the stable, but as the hound was in the loose box and the monkey slept in an adjoining stall, I did not anticipate that they would meet.

All went well—the hound had a good supper and went to sleep without "singing," and later the monkey was taken down to her cage in the stall.

"THEY WERE THE GREATEST PALS"

The next morning I went into the stable and found my monkey had escaped from her box. Peering into the loose box I expected to see a gorged foxhound or certainly the remains of a mangled monkey. Instead, I discovered her, warm and happy, curled up against the hound's "tummy," while Furrier seemed to be enjoying her company.

This was the more extraordinary as the hound was not a particularly friendly one, was a doghound, and had come straight from the hunt kennels, having been hunting until he was sent to me.

I can only surmise that he took the monkey for a friendly human being—for as long as I had him they were the greatest pals—the monkey always sleeping loose in the hound's box.

Furrier cannot have been said to have earned his living during the short time I had him. He sat for me certainly, but if allowed out for a moment he would at once wander off, gaily waving his stern to everyone he met; he would nose his way into the first kitchen door that was open and demolish anything in the way of food that might be about, while the occupants of the room sat aghast or shrieked for the police.

The contents of butchers', poulterers' or fish shops he would take in his stride, and, as the owner of the dog was soon discovered, my household accounts increased enormously in consequence. "Two prime joints taken by the fox dog" became frequent items on my weekly commissariat books.

Gates and doors, unless bolted or firmly latched, never stopped him, and a smell of meals in progress or preparation would bring the foxhound and his gaily waving stern through any open ground-floor window.

Then no shouting or rating would stop him from eating what he had winded. Just pleased he had called, and only a whipper-in's rate or a thong round his loins would have made any impression. Those few weeks he was with me Furrier had the time of his life ; rather a difficult breed of dog to keep in the suburbs of London.

Furrier certainly " got " his living, although perhaps he did not always earn it.

He soon had to return to Essex.

I have mentioned the monkey. Now, she was also a model,

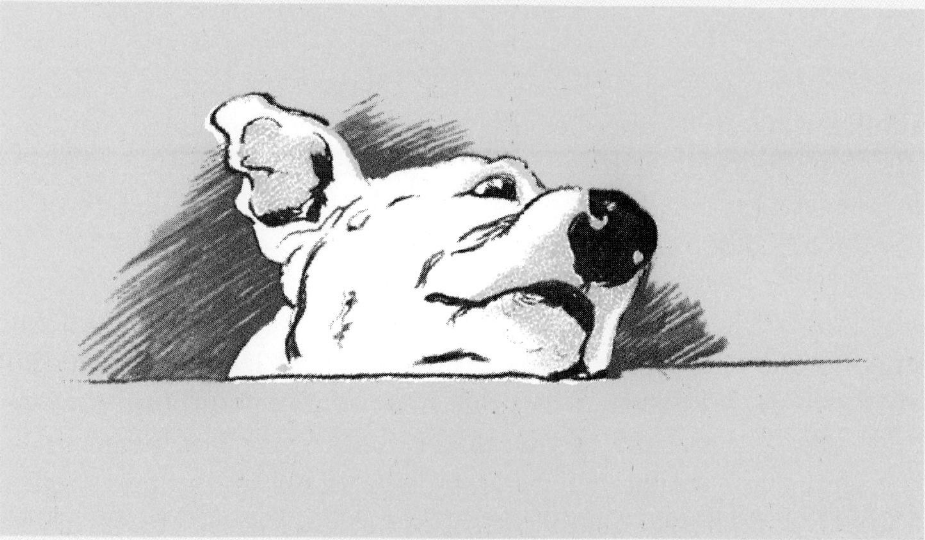

" THIS BOOK IS ABOUT DOGS, NOT MONKEYS, PLEASE "

If Cracker will allow me, may I tell you of her?

Her arrival was dramatic, if nothing else.

One evening, sitting at dinner, not thinking of monkeys or anything pertaining to them, a message came through that a large and savage monkey on a chain was waiting for me at the station, and as none of the station staff would go near it, I was requested by the station-master to " clear " at once.

On inquiry, as no address of the sender was on the label, I endeavoured to persuade him that there was a mistake in the name, and it was not for me; also, that I knew nothing about any monkey and was not expecting one.

He was, however, obdurate. I " must clear and clear at once, as there was no doubt as to the name."

Now an all-of-a-sudden monkey is a little disconcerting to arrange for, especially as I had never previously owned one. However, my wife immediately developed a wish for a monkey, and there was nothing for it but to sally forth and "clear."

On arriving at the station I found an excited group of porters and idlers teasing a 2-ft. green monkey, who was dancing and chattering at the end of a chain attached to her waist. Seeing that I was to be the "bear-leader," I suggested that this teasing should now cease and, leaving the monkey to calm down, and incidentally to get a little jumping powder for myself, I repaired to the station bar, from which place I shortly returned alone to the parcels office to make friends with Sally.

Here I found her dancing the Charleston, or a very good imitation of it, first on one leg and then on the other. Having undone one end of her chain, I attempted to lead her away, but after two or three steps I had this nicely entangled round my legs, and Sally biting hard at my ankles. Grasping her firmly under the chin and tucking her body tightly under my elbow, I made a dash for my home, finally getting her safely housed for the night.

Not for many months afterwards did I discover the sender.

Two years earlier a friend had been in my studio who was shortly going out to West Africa, and at the time I had casually mentioned that a monkey would be an amusing model. On his arrival back in England he had sent the monkey on a chain, addressed to me, either forgetting or, as a practical joke, not advising me of its dispatch, or his arrival in England.

Just a few incidents of her after-career, many of which have to do with my doggy models.

Now, this monkey was in reality a very friendly animal, and had a passion for dogs. In the daytime during the winter she would be chained up to an open chimney-corner in my studio, surrounded by a group of bobtail puppies and full-grown dogs.

These puppies had what are known as wall eyes, i.e. one light eye, or eyes with light specks on them, and these specks and light eyes were an endless source of interest to the inquisitive Sally.

"THIS MAKES US TIRED"

When the puppies were asleep she would very carefully pull open an eyelid—and gaze in wonder at the eye—turning her head first on one side and then on the other as she did so.

Another source of delight to Sally was dog dentistry—for she would very carefully waggle the loose milk teeth of the puppies while they were sleeping, pulling up their lips in the same careful way that she did their eyelids, and gently moving the loose teeth about until one day—much to Sally's interest and delight—they came out in her hand.

I think it really must be that dogs take monkeys' hands for human hands—anyhow, this opening of the sleeping eye and mouth never seemed to wake the puppies.

Another and rather alarming habit Sally had was to push small red-hot cinders from the fire towards the room and carpet. This she did very carefully in short sharp jerks for fear of burning her hands—after every push rubbing her fingers vigorously together. I say alarming, because my carpet (fully insured) suffered, and on one or two occasions, when by accident left alone, she narrowly escaped setting fire to my studio.

Her playing with fire, however, very nearly cost her her life.

One day, when left for a few moments, she must have been " Charlestoning " about on her hind legs as usual, playing with some of the puppies, and somehow or other have swung her chain over the nearest steel fire dog. Then, getting frightened, she only twisted it up more until she was forced by the shortness of her chain to be uncomfortably near the fire itself.

On my return in a few minutes I found her with hands and feet very badly burned.

Getting her loose immediately, I carried her across the room, at the same time calling for a hospital nurse, who happened to be in the house, and soon Sally was in the nurse's lap and her hands were scientifically greased and bandaged. Instead of tearing these off as I fully expected, the monkey did not attempt to do so, and each morning afterwards, when nurse came to freshly bandage and grease, Sally would hold out both hands like a child—never once attempting to tear off the bandages.

The following year I spent the summer at a farmhouse at Maidensgrove in Oxfordshire, and took down my then menagerie by rail.

This consisted of many bobtail sheep-dogs and terriers, with Sally on a coupling chain running with them. A somewhat comical lot for a railway guard to take in his van; they were, no doubt, taken for a collection of performing animals.

Near the farmhouse was a large pond, and, as it was a very hot summer, the bobtails would go for a daily swim, Sally always trotting down with them, but being uncoupled before the dogs dashed into the water.

One hot day she struggled on her lead to go in with her friends, so, attaching a long piece of twine to her waistbelt in case she should sink and have to be hauled out, I let her go. In plunged the bobtails, and rushing with them helter-skelter was the now delighted monkey, spluttering a good deal at first, but soon developing an over-arm side-stroke swimming action. When she got tired she clambered on to the biggest bobtail's back and returned in triumph to the shore.

Always afterwards in hot weather Sally had her swim with the dogs.

Another model I had was a small pink pig. This little fellow was the one of a large litter with whom his mother would have nothing to do. My wife offered to rear him by hand, and he soon learnt to walk out with my children, with the terriers and other dogs, and also stand up on his hind legs and take food from the hand.

He had his own little sty in the yard, and my family attended to all his wants. In time he became almost as domesticated as a dog. Whistle him, and he would come galloping across the yard and follow you anywhere.

One very cold day when my family were returning from their walk, he ran into the house with the terriers and a few seconds later Peter was found sitting up in front of the sitting-room fire surrounded by the dogs and thoroughly enjoying the warmth.

After this it became a habit, and every cold day the children would bring Peter in to the fire to snuggle up with the dogs. There they would all lie in a heap, Peter always getting the best place by using his pink nose to push out of his way any terriers who were there first.

"WHISTLE HIM, AND HE WOULD COME GALLOPING ACROSS THE YARD"

"NONIE"

Still another model of mine was Nonie, a Scotch terrier, a rather well-known canine character during the war, who belonged to a Colonel in the R.A.F.

When this dog came to me to sit he was a very proud personage, wearing all his medals in the form of engraved discs attached to his collar. He had had rather an exciting career, as he was born on H.M.S. *Lion* during the battle of Jutland, and when he was full grown had constantly been "up" bombing over the German lines, had flown the Channel, and been into action in a tank.

A hospital nurse staying in my house vouched for this story of a Scotch terrier and one of her patients. A little girl of about three years old had a Scotch terrier given to her as a birthday present —"for her very own"—and this dog was the child's constant companion. As there is nothing children love more—especially little girls—than "dressing up," Bogie, the Scotch terrier, was constantly attired in the flowing robes of a large baby doll of her owner's. Now, Bogie would sleepily enjoy this dressing up and would afterwards lie at full length in any place in which she was put.

One hot day, when a walk in Hyde Park was indicated, Bogie was taken, dressed up in the doll's clothes, and placed at one end of her owner's perambulator, while the child sat up and watched her at the other end.

Although Bogie was in the " pram," there was very little of her to be seen.

First of all, she had on a tight-fitting baby bonnet tied down under her chin, and below this a long, flowing robe completely hid her hairy body and tail, only her nose and fore feet showing—the latter being pulled through the armholes of the dress. As I have said, Bogie was a lazy person and loved to sleep in warm things more than anything else, but she also—like many Scotch terriers—loved a fight.

In the Broad Walk in Hyde Park are many children and nursemaids and dogs, and on this day a fight had started between a collie and a bull terrier just as the perambulator and its charges arrived.

From all sides people and park keepers rushed to try and separate these two dogs, but no sticks or choking would stop them. Over and over they rolled until, coming close to the perambulator, a black and hairy-faced baby suddenly appeared from its snowy depths, as with one plunge Bogie leapt from the pram, dashing between policemen, boys' and nursemaids' legs as she charged into the fray.

The dignity of her course, however, was sadly marred and impeded by her long dress which tripped her up on her hurried journey towards the two combatants, and made her hind legs more or less useless as galloping appendages.

When two large and pugnacious dogs start a serious fight they are not easy to part. Neither park keeper nor tradesmen's boys were successful in separating them, and it looked as if one of the dogs would soon be badly damaged.

Bogie's advent at once cleared the atmosphere, as the sight of the Scotch terrier's approach, constantly tripping up as she ran towards them, so frightened both the collie and the bull terrier that they immediately forgot their own private quarrel and stampeded in fright in opposite directions.

The child's terrier then took possession of the centre of the arena, her tail quivering with excitement, but still surmounted by the flowing robes, now somewhat soiled and dishevelled.

A very great friend of Cracker and Mick is a small Exmoor pony.

This pony has grown up with these two dogs, and although now five years old is not a great deal taller than Mick, with whom he is very fond of playing.

Their favourite game is hide-and-seek—which is played in this way around my studio which stands in the centre of a grass yard.

Cracker, the clown, generally starts the game by dashing round and round the studio in a mad gallop—pony and dogs immediately giving chase ; suddenly he will slip into reverse, and, dashing round the building the opposite way, meet them all on the other side, immediately doubling back on his tracks and appearing behind them, when the game will begin again in the opposite direction.

This game, with Cracker as " he," is fully understood and entered into by all of them. When they are tired, or Cracker has been caught and duly rolled over by the others, Jackie, the pony, will lie down in the sun and all the dogs will pile up around him, using the pony as a head cushion.

At other times they will all romp around the yard, Cracker and Mick running by Jackie's side and Bogie, the er—er— terrier, hanging on to the pony's long tail.

A third game called " hunt the bone " (all of which I see from my studio window, which accounts for so little work being done) is played as follows :—

Jane, the Airedale, has a habit, reminiscent no doubt of her wild ancestors, of burying any bone in this grass yard she cannot eat up.

Things being otherwise dull, and Cracker having no game to suggest—Jackie will carefully nose round the yard until he locates one of Jane's caches of hidden bones.

With his forehoof he will then proceed to dig until a bone appears upon the surface, while Jane stands barking round him with indignation at her reserve larder being invaded.

The game then starts by Jackie seizing this bone in his mouth and dashing off as " he," Jane and the others giving chase. The end of the game is when the pony flings the bone in the air as a dog would do when playing with it—and Jane recovers her hidden treasure.

I am glad I saved Jackie from being sold to go down the coal mines, for when I bought him he was destined for a life underground.

He has one insatiable longing, and that is to get inside my studio and become an artist's model like the rest.

On one occasion he managed to accomplish this.

My man had been in to light my studio fire and had inadvertently forgotten to latch the door when leaving.

"THEY WILL ALL ROMP AROUND THE YARD"

Returning a short time afterwards he found the pony inside, with his forehoofs on the sofa upon which Cracker and Mick were peacefully reclining. His great treat, however, is to be given sweet table biscuits, which he eats with delight—and will follow you anywhere if you have a sugar biscuit in your hand.

Some years ago there was produced at the Prince of Wales and Strand Theatres, during two consecutive Christmas holiday-tides, a children's play called " The Happy Family," with which I had a great deal to do.

For this play a real dog had to be found to take rather an important part in the cast.

After some trouble a bobtail sheep-dog was discovered who filled the rôle exactly, and who was, moreover, a perfect actor—never once missing his entrance cue, or putting in any "gag" not in the " book."

Jim, for that was his name, lived with Fabia Drake, and for six weeks each year waited in the wings until his entrance cue

"A PERFECT ACTOR"

arrived, barked at the right moment when on the stage, and made his exit at the correct time.

He never seemed to get tired of what, to a dog, must have appeared to be a rather monotonous nightly performance.

If the truth were known, I think he must in reality have been rather proud of playing the lead with Noel Coward, Mimi Crawford, Fabia Drake, and many others who were then children, or boys and girls, playing to almost their first London audience.

It is astonishing how soon animals, even those not specially trained for stage work, will adapt themselves to the glare of the footlights and noises of the orchestra.

At a Gaiety play, in which I had a minor part as designer of the scenery and costumes and the man who superintended the live-stock while in the theatre, whatever his stage name may be, I had to find a pack of hounds, two terriers, four horses, a donkey, and a couple of gamecocks—certainly a mixed bag.

The eight couples of hounds (gifts) were easily procured from some of my hunting friends—and were, I think, the worst eight couples of foxhounds I have ever seen.

Unluckily, at the dress rehearsal one or two had developed, or shall we say had a recurrence of, their old complaint—kennel lameness.

Now—for those who do not know it—kennel lameness is a form of rheumatism.

A hound with this may not feel it when once on the move and warmed up, so to speak; but if waiting in the wings of a theatre for some time, and then being suddenly asked to get up and move on, he will give vent to the most dismal and penetrating howl imaginable—and this is what happened at their first appearance.

From under the stage, in the middle of a tender love passage above them, came that howl of pain as a twinge of rheumatism caught old "Gamester." The producer was frantic with wrath, and I was sent below to get the culprits out of the building as soon as possible.

Luckily, the play did not have a long run, or my pack of hounds would have looked like fat pugs, as every lady member of the chorus would insist upon feeding them the whole time they were in the theatre. In the end a notice had to be put on the official notice board :

"YOU MUST NOT FEED THE ANIMALS."

One night a serious accident might have occurred. As many of my readers know, there is very little room in the wings for a large company of chorus, scene shifters, and principals—to say nothing of a pack of hounds and numerous horses.

All the horses were thoroughly tested as to quietness, and all went well until one night, when something happened to one of our equine staff, and the man who supplied them sent a friend with a fresh horse to take its place.

On going behind I found a very horsey-looking individual trying to steady down an excitable hackney—which I have no doubt he had offered to lend our animal supply man in the hope of getting behind the stage himself.

Now, though scenery may look solid from the front of the house, a horse rearing or plunging against it from behind would probably bring a lot of it down on the performers.

Just as I arrived on the scene "up" went this hackney, his fore-hoofs waving in the air, with the scenery in his vicinity rocking ominously—and he was quickly ordered off with his horsey owner, whom I found explaining to the members of the chorus around him what a perfectly quiet animal his hackney was and how suitable for work on the stage.

In another five minutes the greater part of the scenery on the O.P. side would have crashed.

No ! My friend got "behind," but I am glad to say neither he nor his hackney stayed for the performance.

CHAPTER IV

WHICH TELLS OF SOME THINGS YOU OUGHT TO KNOW, AND OF SOME BAD HABITS

ALL dogs want regular exercise. Never keep a dog chained up without, at least, one daily run off the chain.

Puppies and young dogs often have a fit—this is not rabies.

If your puppy has a fit, shut him up in a quiet place until recovered; never put him with other dogs, as they are sure to bite him.

For very small dogs a padded clothes basket is a very good thing for this purpose.

At the time of writing there is no case of rabies in England, although lots of puppies are having fits.

There is no danger to the human being in handling a dog in a fit.

Many young puppies have inhabitants both inside and out.

If a puppy's coat stares, i.e. stands up on end, and he looks thin and poor, he probably has worms.

In this case he may eat voraciously one day and refuse food the next. Ruby mixture is the best cure I know. For outside parasites, Spratts' dog soap.

In training a dog use as few words as possible—each word meaning to the dog a particular thing he has to do. Always use the same word for the same required action—say it distinctly, sharply, and clearly.

Cars make many dogs sick when they first journey in them—watch out if in your own car, and try very short journeys first.

A puppy under four months should never be tied up to a kennel.

A dog who kills cats is a nuisance to his master and—the cats.

A dog on a lead is more likely to want to fight others if you drag him away from every dog he meets.

"DON'T DRAG HIM AWAY FROM EVERY DOG HE MEETS"

If your dog looks like being run over by a car, don't call him if he has his back towards you and the car is facing him. If you do so he will probably look round at you and not see the car.

No dog that was ever whelped can grow up without some faults which have to be corrected—but, to the owner, the most expensive of these faults is for him to develop a taste for chasing sheep or cattle.

Cattle- and sheep-worrying occur more often with the larger breeds of dogs, but any dog who shows the slightest sign of doing this should always be corrected in the firmest and most drastic way possible.

It is almost impossible to cure an old and confirmed sheep-worrier, but luckily there are not many of them, as they generally die a sudden and quick death at the hands of their owners in the earlier stages of their existence.

Apart from the unpleasant side of the performance to the harmless sheep, the actual cost of but one sheep-worrying bout among a flock of ewes may easily run the dog owner into damages amounting to hundreds of pounds. All dog owners do not seem to realize this fact.

If you have a dog who worries sheep and you wish to keep him, the only thing to do is to live in London or some large town, and never take him out of it, and even then never take him near sheep in Hyde Park. The safest plan, however, is to have him humanely destroyed.

I have seen ladies with a little terrier or toy dog allow him to chase sheep and even encourage him to do so.

A large dog, of course, does much more damage—but even a little toy, if allowed to frighten a flock of in-lamb ewes, may let his owner in for a heavy damage bill.

Any large dog, when he first sees cattle or sheep, should be watched very carefully—and at the slightest inclination to chase them should be immediately rated. If this inclination is very apparent, i.e. the dog's hackles go up—a good plan is to have about ten yards of very strong cord, attaching one end to his collar and the other end to yourself. Then take him among them, having a serviceable hunting crop with you.

If he starts after them, rate him well, but if he does not stop, let him run the length of the cord and then throw the full weight of your body on your end as he pulls it taut.

This, as he is not expecting it, thinking he has got away, will probably pull him over and will give him a severe shock which he won't forget in a hurry, and the soundest hiding you can then give him will be an additional aid to memory.

It is, of course, a drastic plan, but the disease needs one, and is a case of " spare the rod and spoil the child," remembering all the time that the confirmed sheep-worrier has to be destroyed in the end.

A dog that kills poultry is another expensive hobby. I once had one; he was given to me with that character, and he certainly lived up to it.

All went well while my home was in London, but when I went to live in the country he killed seven lusty hens in the first two days, having a real good whip-hiding after each bout. Hens and cats he would kill as if they were mice.

To try and stop his chicken-killing propensities I kept him for a week chained up in a farmyard where poultry swarmed, thinking that probably he would get used to them, being surrounded by them night and day; also every day he was exercised on a lead among them. At the end of a week I decided to let him loose for his walk round the yard, but the moment he was off the lead he caught a hen and, before he could be stopped, killed her.

Then for some days he had this dead chicken tied to his collar, but that also was a hopeless failure—although it must have been excessively uncomfortable, being tied close up to his neck.

After trying every remedy for chicken killing I had heard of, I had to own myself beaten; and as I had to keep John Hogg (for that was his name) in the country, his death-warrant was signed.

The morning I did this I had to go to London, and, meeting a friend in town, told him about the dog. Luckily for John Hogg, this friend had for some time been looking for a dog to keep in town, and he offered to take him if we could get a wire through in time to stop his execution.

Rushing to the nearest telegraph office I hastily sent one off, and I shall never forget the horror on the face of the telegraph operator when she read the message:

"Don't shoot John Hogg today."

After this narrow escape he lived with my friend in London for many years.

And here let me tell you a story of an egg-stealing dog.

Some doggy friends of mine in Warwickshire, whose garden adjoined their farmyard, were very perturbed because suddenly, for no known reason, their supply of eggs seemed to be going astray.

The daughter of the house, who undertook the daily collecting of these eggs from the various mangers and hiding places where the laying hens usually deposited their embryo offspring, suddenly found them missing in many of her charges' most cherished and secluded places. Various theories were suggested as the cause of this, and suspicion certainly attached itself to youthful members of the staff.

Now, this family had also a number of four-footed companions, many of whom daily accompanied the egg collector on her rounds, and one of these was a retriever. Weeks went by and the egg supply still continued to grow less, although it was the height of the laying season; but it was also noticed that the retriever was getting inordinately fat, and his evening meal did not seem to tempt him very much. Also, he spent most

"AT THE END OF A WEEK I DECIDED TO LET HIM LOOSE"

of his day sitting on the lawn, from which place he would make sudden excursions towards the farmyard, barns, and outbuildings, obviously with some very compelling reason.

At breakfast, after this had been discussed, the daughter of the house determined to watch and follow him in order to find out what was the reason of the dog's constant journey farmyard-wards. So that morning she took a book on to a quiet corner of the stoop surrounding one side of the house and, when our friend the retriever took up his position in the centre of the lawn, kept a careful look out.

The dog, however, seemed restless, although not moving away, his ears forward all the while as if listening for the footsteps of a friend or master.

Presently a distant " cluck, cluck, cluck, cluck-ut," repeated two or three times, came from the farmyard, and the retriever immediately got up, left his place on the lawn, and walked towards the farm buildings nearby—followed at a distance by the watcher.

On arriving at the farmyard he was seen to make a careful inspection of all the secret laying places where eggs had previously been deposited and to which with his young mistress he had constantly been taken before, in the morning and evening egg rounds. At one of these a warm, freshly-laid egg was found—and this the retriever quickly demolished.

Having eaten the egg and well-licked his paws he returned to his post on the lawn, at once taking up his original listening attitude.

Although his mistress had caught him red-handed egg stealing, she had a keen sense of humour; so coming quietly back to the stoop again, she also took up her position to watch for further developments. Half an hour went by, the day was hot, and the dog at last dozed—or so it seemed to the girl. Then once more on the still air came the well-known " cluck, cluck, cluck-ut " from the farmyard, and the dog, as if hit with a stick, jumped to his feet listening, and the same egg-finding process was repeated as before. Six or eight eggs were found and eaten in this way during the morning. Whenever the bell rang—the " cluck, cluck, cluck-ut " of the newly-made mother hen—the listening retriever knew that a nice hot meal was ready.

It is the extraordinary way in which this dog must have connected the clucking of the hen with the preparing of a meal for himself, and then deliberately set out to find it, which induces me to give you this story.

How he discovered this except by some reasoning process, it is impossible to tell, but there is no doubt that he did reason it out, or instinctively connect it with egg laying, as when listening

"TAKING UP HIS ORIGINAL LISTENING ATTITUDE"

on the lawn he would always at once go in the direction from which the "cluck" of the hen came—his strategic listening position being in the centre of the egg-laying area.

Years before I had Mickey I owned another large dog. I will not mention the breed as I am sure my Irish wolfhound would not wish me to do so. This bitch was the sweetest tempered lady imaginable, but she had one failing, and that was . . . goats. Now, whether goats smell like—whatever it was her ancestors used to hunt—I do not know, but goats, even the "winding" of a goat, put her hackles up immediately.

The first time I discovered this was when I was asked if one of the goats kept at the Hunt kennels adjoining my house might be put for a day into my studio grass yard.

When the goat was brought down, he was the ugliest, hairiest, raggedest billy-goat imaginable, one you could wind a mile away.

When Biddy, the bitch I am speaking about, came out of the house towards the high gate of the yard, I noticed that she immediately put her nose in the air, and her hackles went up like the business side of a wire brush. This, of course, was a warning to me that there might be trouble if she met the goat, but in trying to step through the gate to my studio and shut her safely outside she pushed by me, got into the yard, and the trouble immediately commenced, as she at once dashed straight at his withers and tried to pull him down.

I rated—I cursed—but seeing she had quite " gone wild " and would certainly kill that goat if she could, I yelled to a friend in the house to come and help me.

Biddy, meanwhile, might have been a mad thing for all the notice she took of my voice or whip, and no efforts of ours could catch either the dog or the goat, who with his pursuer was all this time rushing round and round my yard in circles.

We then decided to open the narrow gate, hoping that the goat in his mad fright would charge through, and so allow us to catch Biddy as she passed.

In the end this ruse was successful, for although my friend missed the dog I managed to get hold of her round the quarters and hang on as they both dashed through the gateway together, while a bloody goat went tearing down the tarmac road to the village as if the hounds of hell were behind him.

Now the thing to remember is, that this bitch was the sweetest tempered and quietest dog possible, and took no notice of sheep, cattle, or any other animal, her only failing being . . . goats.

Remember, that even the quietest dog may have one dislike.

"DASHED STRAIGHT AT HIS WITHERS"

The bigger the breed of dog, the more careful his owner should be with his education as he grows up, and should always watch out for anything of this sort.

I have known dog owners who consider their dogs clever and good guard dogs if they growl at visitors when inside the house. This is a bad fault. Visitors who are good enough for the master should be good enough for his dog, provided they do not tease or otherwise annoy the animal, and no barking should be allowed when once a visitor has been admitted.

A small Pekinese of my acquaintance has a habit, like so many of them, of continuing to yap long after friends of his mistress have settled down in the house, even continuing to do so in his master's and mistress's presence. That is a badly-trained dog; he is very old now, but this fault should have been corrected in his youth. My system of silencing him is a very simple one.

I discovered by experience that, notwithstanding his ferocious bark, owing to his great age he had lost almost all his teeth, which had rendered his bite perfectly harmless, so I sat down beside him and allowed him to bite at my hand without drawing it away. When I did this he soon stopped barking and biting, and we became, if not friends, at least acquaintances not worth barking at—a sort of armed neutrality.

I once saw a very old Peke that had had monkey glands injected, and it was a most pathetic sight—a poor little wizened, shrivelled-up, grey-muzzled pet, trying to play and romp like a puppy.

I had been contemplating monkey glands for myself, but after seeing that Peke . . . I have changed my mind. Better a sedate old age than a hectic latter end.

Another fault of the owner, if not of the dog, is overfeeding.

Believe me, it is no pleasure to the dog to be so fat that he can hardly waddle—to say nothing of liver and other troubles that arise from it and make his life miserable. One good meal at night, and vimlets, hound meal, or a dog biscuit or two in the morning, for the larger breeds, is far the best diet for a healthy, full-grown dog—as long as he can always get water should he want it.

The quantity of food given, of course, depends entirely upon the size of your dog.

Another habit which should not be encouraged is for your dog to jump up at you and put his forepaws on your dress.

You may not object to it, but your visitors will certainly do so in muddy weather. A dog should always be taught to stay "down" when he is told to; neither should he be allowed to curl up upon any piece of furniture for which he has a fancy. His own dog basket should be available for this purpose.

Running after motor-cycles or cars is another very dangerous habit in young dogs—if allowed to do this they never live long—and should at once be corrected; besides, it is an unpleasant and skiddy pastime for the motorist or motor-cyclist.

If you live in the country, a dog who goes hunting on his own, unless the coverts are your property, will lead a precarious existence.

Some day a keeper will put a dose of shot into him which will stop his hunting for ever. Who is to know if a dog that is constantly poaching is one day shot and buried in the wood where he falls ?

He may be let off once or twice, but he is bound to disappear in the end. Besides this, he is causing a considerable amount of ill-feeling between you and your neighbours.

"HE IS BOUND TO DISAPPEAR IN THE END"

Two dogs are much more liable to develop this habit than one, and one confirmed poacher will soon persuade another dog to help him.

A friend of mine has a couple of terriers very fond of hunting rabbits, etc.

If both are loose together they will immediately sneak off to the woods, but by keeping them alternately on the chain and never letting both out together he has found a remedy; neither of them caring to go off alone.

Only a few days ago I heard of two dogs at Thames Ditton who, when loose together, would " go for " every other dog in the vicinity, but when let out one at a time were perfectly friendly, or at any rate did not fight, with the other canine residents of the neighbourhood.

MY ALSATIAN FRIEND.

I do not wish to enter into any controversy as to the Alsatian, never having owned one myself, although I have known many of them.

But we must remember that there are at the moment probably more Alsatians in England than any other breed of large dog—and in consequence a larger proportion of both good and bad characters. Also today, if anyone gets bitten by an Alsatian, the whole world hears of it through the newspapers.

The Alsatian is a highly nervous dog and, although fond of his master, does not make friends quickly.

AN ALSATIAN WHO LOOKED VERY LIKE A WOLF.

Some weeks ago I made the acquaintance of an Alsatian who looked very much like a wolf, but this dog certainly had an exceptionally nice disposition. He was with me in a room for three whole days while I made studies from him—and we were the greatest friends, although total strangers before; but no doubt, as in all breeds—there are Alsatians *and* Alsatians.

Any shy-natured dog will easily become what is known as bad-tempered if improperly handled and educated.

"LIE DOWN, CRACKER"

Even Cracker might soon develop a desire to " go " for his master if ill-treated.

In my employ is a Scotch gardener who has no knowledge of dogs and their ways, notwithstanding that he has been with me for many years.

Now, although if a savage or nervous dog attempts to bite you it is a good plan to stand still, it is also wise to *speak* to him at once in a friendly and doggy way.

On the other hand, whenever my gardener meets any of my dogs he will stand perfectly motionless and never utter a sound. This always gives dogs the " nerves," and in consequence every dog of mine, until corrected, always barks at him.

They do not dislike him, but he just gives them the " nerves."

Once, when sketching in Leicestershire, I drove my car into a farmyard, intending to leave it there for an hour or two. As I stepped out of it I saw a large retriever, with hackles up,

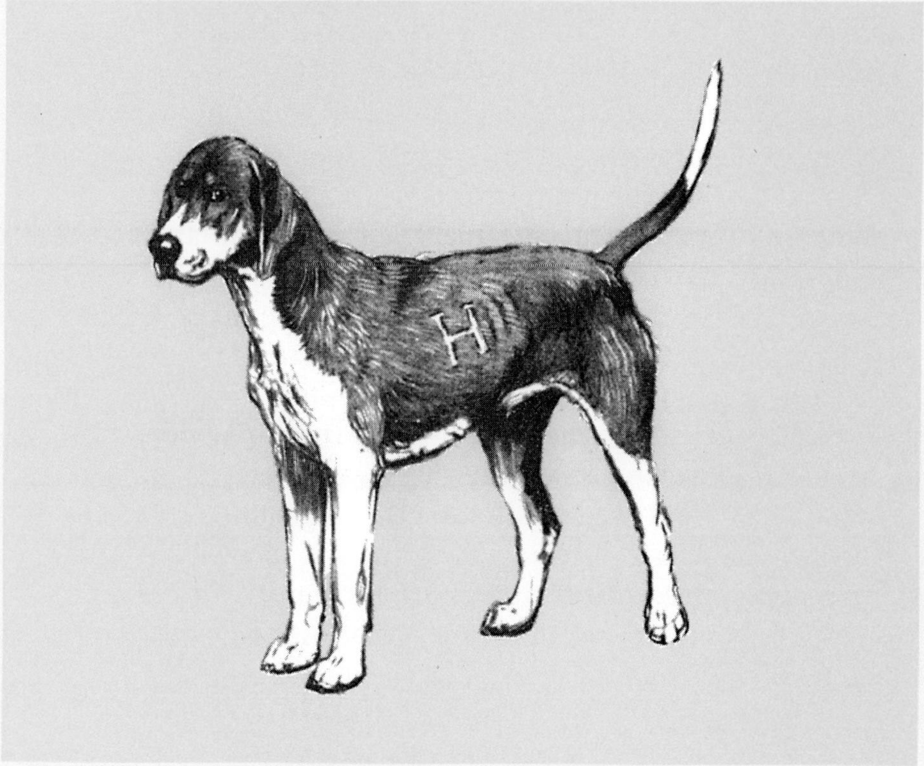

A FRENCH STAGHOUND.

rushing towards me. He was too close to allow me time to gracefully step back into my car again and shut the door upon him. There was only one thing to do—stand still and try to soothe his wrath by friendly talk; I could see, however, that he meant "business," as his white teeth were bared ready for action, and, if the truth were known, I was probably petrified with fright. This petrification, I think, saved me from being seriously bitten.

Dashing up to me, the dog took a firm hold of the calf of my leg, and I expected to see him taking a juicy morsel back to his kennel for later consumption.

Although perspiration streamed from my brow in cupfuls, I automatically continued speaking to him in a friendly and ingratiating manner, and to my infinite relief his teeth did not come *together* through my leg—they did not even break the skin. As I did not move it he presently relaxed his hold and walked away, but had I attempted to run, shout at him, or threaten him, it is certain he would have bitten me severely. By not dragging my leg away I probably saved myself from walking on one real and one timber leg for the rest of my life.

When hunting in France some years ago I had an even worse fright of this description. I had gone one afternoon to make some sketches at the Forêt d'Halatte Hunt kennels, and for the purpose of making these was seated in one of the yards with about ten couples of the big French hounds sitting and lying on the benches opposite to me. By my side stood one of the kennelmen with a whip who saw that the hounds stayed up on their benches. All went well until some little distance away the bell of the kennels clanged, clanged again, and then a few minutes afterwards clanged a third time more insistently.

Muttering something in French that Alfonse was away and that he must answer the gate, my assistant hurried out, pulling the kennel door shut and leaving me seated inside.

And here, for those who do not know the French staghounds, I should like to describe them, and will try to do so with truth and not as they appeared to me at that moment.

The French hound is bigger and more leggy than the English foxhound, sometimes tricolour, but often " bleu " in colour, being almost all over a blue-grey like a German boarhound. Moreover, they have not that kind and friendly expression that our English foxhounds have ; at any rate, they did not seem to have it as I looked up at them from my work on hearing that kennel door shut.

Ten couples of these great brutes sitting up a few yards away with forty eyes fixed upon me made me feel very wobbly about the knees. Here again, being too frightened to do anything else, the only thing to do was to sit still and continue—sketching.

At the end of a few minutes—which seemed to me hours—the kennelman returned, full of apologies for forgetting I was shut in the kennel and for leaving me when he went to open the gates.

This is the sketch of a French hound as I made it at the time.

Which also reminds me of the true story of a M.F.H. who once resided in my house.

A question had arisen with the authorities with regard to the number of licences taken out—whether they were adequate for the hounds in kennel? Our Master (perhaps because he had a doubt about this himself) suggested that the best way for both sides would be for the excise officer to come to the kennels and count them—" round about sixty couples." A day and time was fixed, and the officer, knowing nothing of the management or handling of hounds, duly arrived and was at once taken by the Master into one of the yards—where, on his instructions, the whole pack was waiting to be counted. " There," said the Master as he pushed his visitor gently but firmly through the gate, " now you can count them yourself, and we can soon settle it." " Round about sixty couples " of hounds would not be easy for an expert to count, even if jogging along a road, but in a small yard with two specially instructed kennelmen seeing to it that they " kept moving," it was an impossibility.

" NOW YOU CAN COUNT THEM YOURSELF "

Our friend, the inspector, made many starts with the help (?) of the M.F.H., but when the latter suggested that he (the inspector) should wait in the yard and finish his count alone while the kennel staff made ready for " feeding," the inspector at once agreed that a mistake had arisen, and that no doubt the return was perfectly correct.

One hears many stories of the homing instinct of animals, but these two are worth recording.

Some years ago I purchased some draft, unentered hounds from the Whaddon Chase kennels, i.e. young hounds of one year who have never been hunted, and they were sent by rail, in what are known as crates, from Leighton Buzzard to Reading.

At my kennels there was a grass yard with six-foot wire fencing surrounding it, and the day after their arrival they were put out in this yard.

On my kennel huntsman going out to look at them later, he found one missing and, after a careful inspection of the fencing, discovered at one place that the wire mesh had been bent at the top, showing that some animal had scrambled over it.

Every inquiry was made in the surrounding district, and a letter was sent to the huntsman of the Whaddon, saying that one hound had got away. As it had their ear mark upon it, it was possible that it might be returned to them.

Three days later we had a letter from Leighton Buzzard to say that the puppy had returned to their kennels that afternoon.

As the crow flies, the distance from the two places would only be about 40 miles, but the Thames would have to be crossed, and of course an unentered puppy could not possibly know a yard of the country.

An old hound might have soon got into country he knew, i.e. his own foxhunting country, which in this case would begin as soon as he got to Aylesbury; but to a puppy that had been a year at "walk" almost every yard must have been unknown.

The other case of the homing instinct which has come under my actual knowledge also happened some time ago, and in connection with a rough-haired terrier of mine named Turk—an extraordinarily active and hard little fellow, and very fond of horses. In those days there were a dozen or more road coaches daily starting from Northumberland Avenue at 11 o'clock each morning, and to one of the subscribers to the Boxhill and Dorking coach I had given Turk.

It was, of course, in the days before motors, and the new owner of the dog wanted him to run with the coach on one or two stages every few days, which he could easily do, the idea being for Turk to live at any of the stables where a change of horses was made. I took him up to Northumberland Avenue one morning in May, handed him over to the guard of the Boxhill coach and saw him safely shut up in the inside, it being arranged that as he was new to his surroundings he should travel to Boxhill as an inside passenger, making friends with his new owner when he arrived, and also getting used to the coach stables and his new home.

"I SAW TURK DRAG HIMSELF UNDER THE GATE"

The next day I had a note from my friend saying that the dog had slipped his collar when they took him out of the coach on arrival at Boxhill, and had disappeared.

Nothing was heard of him for some days, although every inquiry was made at the homes for lost dogs and from the police.

At the end of a week we came to the conclusion that he must have been taken in by somebody and kept, for he was a very friendly terrier who would soon get acclimatized to a new home.

Ten days afterwards I was sitting in my garden at Chiswick when I saw a very emaciated and footsore Turk drag himself under the gate.

The dog was so tired and thin that I had serious doubts as to his getting over the terrible time he must have been through. The pads to his feet were raw and the nails worn down to the quick, while his ribs were standing out from his sides like a toast rack.

After that I had not the heart to give him away again, and he lived with me the rest of his life.

Here again the distance, as the crow flies, is not very great, but considering that the dog travelled to Boxhill inside the coach and then found his way back to Chiswick, certainly across one corner of London, it was rather wonderful, although nothing compared to some of the stories one hears of dogs, cats, and other animals travelling half across England. These two, however, have actually come under my own knowledge.

A CHOW.

Have you ever noticed the London chow? The way he stalks about on his own, and is always to be found in certain of London's busy thoroughfares? In Sackville Street I have a chow acquaintance who is always to be found sunning himself on the pavement on a fine day, and in Half Moon Street another is generally to be seen. Then there is the " bomnible dog," as my grandson calls him, always in Westbourne Terrace—another chow. The independent way in which a chow walks alone in London streets makes me give this story. I will give it to you as my friend (the owner of the dog) told it to me.

BACK TO THE WILD IN BIRMINGHAM

" Sun-Yat-Sen was a black chow, and was given to me during the war when I was doing duty in the Isle of Wight. In October 1917 I had to return to barracks at Dover, but when later, at a day's notice, I rejoined my battalion in France, Sunny, my chow, was taken by a friend to my mother's house at Birmingham, and I wondered how soon he would settle down, as he was not a dog to make friends quickly. Later I heard that, on the second day after his arrival, he had jumped from a first-floor window and escaped.

" Every endeavour had been made to find him, and on one or two occasions he was seen by my sisters, who did their utmost to recapture him, constantly stalking him through the busiest streets in Birmingham. Sunny, however, had no intention of being captured by anyone. Knowing how fond I was of the dog, my mother offered a reward to anybody who could catch him, and, as he was soon well known to the police, she hoped that this would have the desired effect.

" From time to time for some weeks she heard of him from the police. Once he was almost caught in a blind alley, but jumped a 5-ft. gate to avoid his pursuers, and then she heard that he had been run over by a taxi and badly hurt, but managed to crawl away before anyone could get hold of him.

" It came also to my sister's knowledge that he sometimes slept on a rubbish heap outside Edgbaston, and at other times on a certain doorstep in one of Birmingham's busiest streets.

" The police made many attempts to secure him, but even if apparently fast asleep he would always be on his feet and away before anyone could catch hold of him. After some months of this vagabond life one of my family found out that a girl in a confectioner's shop, in a poorer part of the town, was regularly feeding him, putting down at a certain time every day outside her shop a plate with scraps upon it.

" She, it appeared, had never been able to handle him, and he would only feed at the plate if she stood away a few yards. Sunny had turned into a complete pariah dog.

" On hearing of this my mother gave the girl 5s. a week to continue feeding him, and in this way he lived wild in Birmingham through the complete winter of 1917–18.

" In June 1918 I got my next leave and, on arrival in England, hastened to Birmingham. The first morning I was at my mother's house I rose early and, having heard overnight full details of Sunny's habits, set out for the confectioner's shop mentioned before.

" I had heard that he usually arrived in the early morning soon after seven, and his plate of food was generally put out by his kind friend directly she was down, she standing a few yards away while he devoured it.

" A few minutes before seven I took up my stand in the passage and presently saw a thin and ragged-coated black dog come sniffing and shambling round the corner which led to the back entrance of the shop. Then, unseen, I watched him eat his food, watched him glance suspiciously from side to side between each mouthful, and noticed that he was still badly limping upon one hind leg, the result of the taxi episode.

" I could see that there would be great difficulty to catch hold of him if he did not recognize me, so, stepping quietly from my hiding-place, I walked *away* from him, at the same time giving

" I WATCHED HIM EAT HIS FOOD "

my old whistle and a ' Come along, Sunny,' in the hope that he would follow.

" On hearing my voice his ears went forward and he looked up, sniffed in my direction, and as I repeated my call came slowly shambling behind me.

" So I walked the two miles to Edgbaston, the dog showing no further sign of recognition, only a dim, hazy remembrance of my voice and whistle. Every time I stopped he did the same a yard or two away, never once allowing me to pat him.

" Having followed me inside the house, and seeing that I made no attempt to catch hold of him, he began to come close to me and sniff my legs.

" Gradually recognition began to dawn upon him, and after an hour alone with me his old friendliness started very slowly to come back, and the hunted expression began to leave his face, and by the following day he was almost the affectionate dog I had left behind me in 1917.

"For the next four years he lived a happy life with me, but his wild period left one characteristic which could never afterwards be eradicated. Nothing would induce him to sleep indoors at night if he could possibly get outside. He would sleep in the porch, in a shed in the garden, any old place of his own choosing, but never in a room if he could avoid it.

"The ultimate passing of Sunny was the saddest part of his life-story.

"During these last four years we lived at Hindhead, on the main Portsmouth Road, and the chow, after his Birmingham traffic experiences, was considered unlikely to be run over by any known make of road nuisance.

"Sunny was as safe as a policeman. He would stand at his own drive gate and watch the cars whirl by without taking any risks or chances.

"On his own gravelled sanctuary he knew quite well that he had nothing to fear, but that, once on the tarmac, the danger would begin. His favourite place was to lie in the sun at this gravelled entrance and watch the traffic rush by. One hot day he was standing in this favourite place when a procession of high-powered racing cars came along.

"Just as one of them was going by my drive at a high rate of speed the one behind tried to cut in and pass him, but not allowing himself, or not being allowed, room enough by the forward car, he swerved off the tarmac up on to Sunny's gravelled sweep, hitting my dog and killing him instantly. Little did they know, those callous murderers, what a pal they had destroyed, as (perhaps luckily for them) they did not even stop to see what damage they had done."

"Thou who passest on the path, if haply thou dost mark this monument, laugh not, I pray thee, tho' it is a dog's grave; tears fell for me, and the dust was heaped upon me by a master's hand."—*From the Greek.*

CHAPTER V

WHICH TELLS YOU ALL ABOUT DOG SHOWS AND OF CRACKER'S GREAT INVENTION

I WONDER which advice you took of mine when I told you in my prologue how to get a dog. Whether you purchased one from the Battersea Dogs' Home, or procured a dog from a known breeder ?

In either case, after attending a dog show you will very probably have come to the conclusion that your own pet is more beautiful than any of the show specimens exhibited, and may therefore wish to enter him for exhibition.

Having made this decision, the first thing to do is to settle in your own mind the breed of your dog, which, if he comes from Battersea, may be somewhat intricate.

Do not let this deter you.

If you go to a large dog show you will see a few breeds where even your Battersea companion may not disgrace you, for you might enter him in the Corgi dog, or the border terrier classes.

There is one difficulty which may stop you showing your "dogs'-home" specimen, and that is that every dog must be registered at the Kennel Club before being exhibited.

To get him registered you must write to the Secretary of the Kennel Club, pay one shilling, and give the dog's pedigree—but in Corgi dog classes they might accept "pedigree unknown." As a last resource you always have Cracker's great annual dog show—where no registration is necessary.

We know the professions of medicine, law, painting, music, etc., but few people know of the latest profession—the professional dog trimmer and "handler."

A CORGI DOG.

If you are showing a dog and have no previous experience of either judges or the show ring yourself, it is necessary to have him taken into the ring by a professional "handler," often of the female sex.

These ladies know exactly when to attract a dog's attention and how to show his points when the judge's eye dwells upon him. They will place their delicate hands behind a West Highlander's six inches of tail and keep it erect in the exact position required, to impress the judge at the moment that he looks at the dog; will make your bloodhound so pucker his face that he looks one mass of wrinkles, and your Dalmatian have more spots on his body than you ever realized. These little touches, combined with the pathetic eyes and pretty upturned face of the "handler," must have an effect on any judge, especially if he is young and of the opposite sex.

Tom Newman, the Duke of Beaufort's huntsman, would make a most wonderful professional dog show "handler." Anyone who has seen him show hounds at Peterborough Foxhound Show will agree with me in this, for in the ring he holds his hounds' undivided attention. I also think he would have rivalled Pavlova, had he taken up stage dancing. On the opposite page are some of the poses by which he keeps his hounds' attention when showing them.

Then your dog must be prepared for show, and by prepared I do not necessarily mean fattened up, although in some sporting breeds to win prizes you must show a fat dog and not a fit one.

After attending a show you will soon see that most of the rough-haired terrier breeds want a lot of time and artistry expended on them before they are "fit for show," all of which is in reality "faking," almost all the hair being plucked from one part of the body and brushed up and coaxed to look long on other parts.

It is useless to show a rough fox terrier, Sealyham or Airedale, unless properly and professionally prepared and "handled." In the ring there is the great art of catching the judge's eye at the right moment for your dog, and the dog's eye at the right moment for the judge. All of which may be missed by the unprofessional exhibitor.

You may be disheartened after reading all this about dog showing, but, once again, do not let it deter you; for Cracker tells me he has invented a machine which will completely do away with the necessity of having a professional "handler" at dog shows, and which has a great advantage for the exhibitor, in that all the spare parts can be procured at very moderate cost at any of Messrs. Woolworth's stores.

TOM NEWMAN AT THE PETERBOROUGH SHOW.

By placing Cracker's apparatus (patent applied for from the Kennel Club) over your dog—in reality, by placing your dog in it—while in the ring, any offending part of the body of the animal can be so manipulated and fixed at the exact shape or angle that a dog-show judge has in his eye, that all human " handling " will be unnecessary.

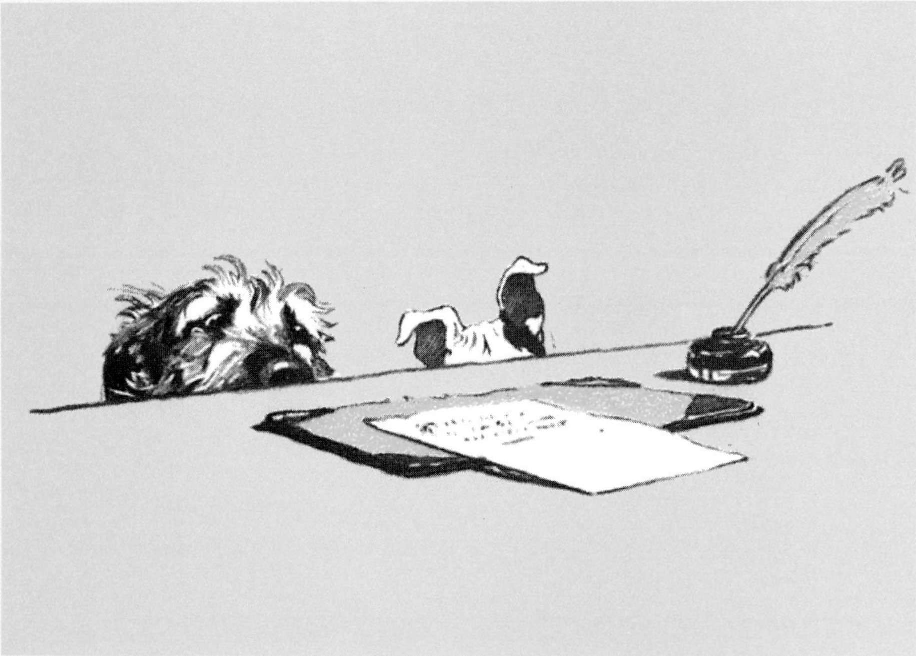

" DON'T BE BASHFUL, CRACKER "

Dog owners will at once realize from the pictures I have made of it, under the personal supervision of the inventor, how useful this will be to exhibitors of bull terriers with curly tails, Aberdeens who carry their tails down, and collies who carry them up, while to all terrier men it will be a *necessity*. Your smooth- or curly-coated Sealyhams can easily be shown in the ring, rough or out of curl, and your Kerry blue beards can by it be elongated to their fullest extent. Even by using this wonderful " dog handler " your Battersea-bought dog may soon become a champion.

Before showing you a working drawing and telling you all this, I have warned Cracker that I am giving away his secrets. I am possibly giving them away to the kennel clubs of the world, but as he continues to wag his tail I must presume he agrees.

On the following two pages I give you (with apologies to my brother artist, Heath Robinson) working designs of his invention which, he tells me, will soon bring dog showing to a

"THE INVENTOR AND 'FRIEND'"

fine art, and revolutionize the profession of dog "handler." Although myself not entirely agreeing with Cracker, there is no doubt in the minds of many of us (that is, the general public) who attend dog shows that human "handling" and trimming for the judging ring has almost reached its limit, if it has not already in some breeds overstepped that mark; and there are many judges who privately disagree with exhibitors having their dogs' tails held by the "handler" at the approved angle, or their fox terriers so squared up at stern and bows that a long-backed dog can almost be made to look like a short-backed one whenever the judge's eye falls upon him.

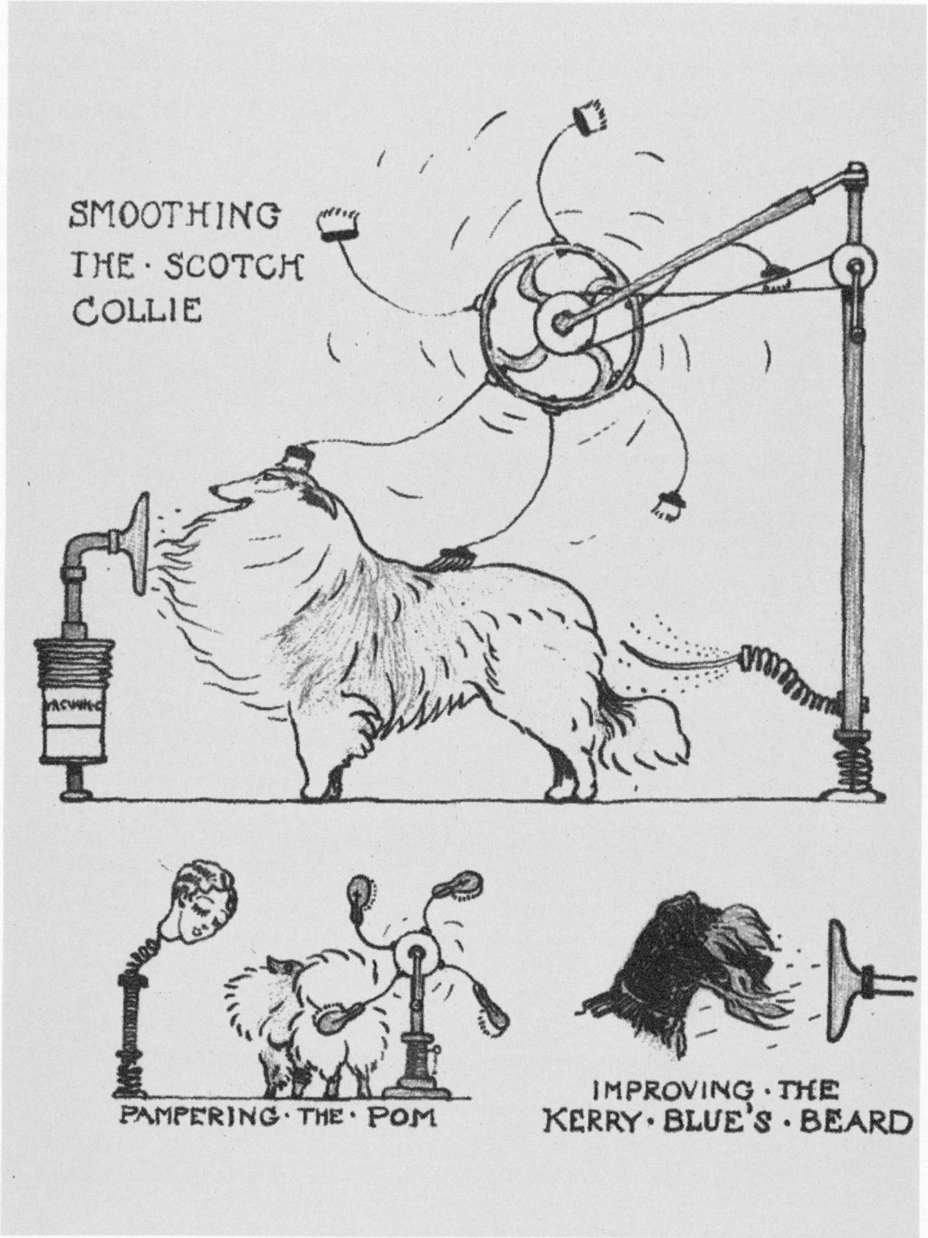

SMOOTHING THE SCOTCH COLLIE

SHOW-RING "HANDLERS"

A very good new edict from the Kennel Club would be: "Hands off your dog while in the ring," the only hand that should touch the dog being that of the judge.

With regard to plucking and singeing, a sister art of the professional "handler," it is now almost possible to alter the actual shape of the dog if the operator is an expert, and even a novice like myself can turn, as I will show you, Bogie, my er—er— terrier, into a show one.

A few days ago a breeder and exhibitor of fox terriers was in my studio and, seeing my er—er— terrier, asked me what I thought she was, which was certainly rather insulting to Bogie.

I at once explained to him that I called her an er—er— terrier, to which he heartily agreed.

The next day I attended another bobbed and shingled dog show, at the Crystal Palace, and, after careful study of the various breeds of terriers, decided that Bogie should be trimmed into a wire-haired fox terrier.

Having purchased at the show the various implements and materials, I got to work on her and, being a bit of a sculptor, soon had her looking like a champion wire-haired terrier.

On opposite page I give two sketches of her:

(*a*) Bogie as an er—er— terrier;

(*b*) The same after shingling and bobbing;

both of which show what can be done, if one starts on virgin soil and if one is not hampered by any Kennel Club regulation as to "faking and trimming," if any such now exist.

In Regent Street, years ago, I saw a Dudley-nosed terrier puppy very quickly converted into the orthodox black-nosed animal.

A dog dealer was standing on the island in the centre of Piccadilly Circus trying to sell to passers-by a couple of puppies which he was carrying, one under each arm. Business was not very brisk and he was chatting to his pal, the owner of an adjoining shoe-black establishment, when a passing lady cast longing eyes at one of the Dudley-nosed puppies.

"BOGIE AS AN ER—ER— TERRIER"

"THE SAME AFTER SHINGLING AND BOBBING"

After some haggling with the seller, when the pink instead of black on the dog's nose was pointed out to her by her male attendant, the deal did not materialize and the couple passed on.

A moment afterwards the dog dealer leant down towards his friend the boot-black and by the simple process of dipping a grimy finger into his blacking pot and rubbing the result well into the offending parts, quickly transformed each Dudley-nose into one of shining black.

Now, before giving any opinion at a dog show as to the judges' awards, I always first wet my finger and rub it well on the prizewinners' noses.

ALL DRESSED UP AND READY FOR THE SHOW RING

The Author-Artist thanks his two friends for their invaluable assistance to him in the preparation of this book. *C. A.*

APPENDIX

SOME DOG CLUBS AND THEIR SECRETARIES

THE AFGHAN HOUND CLUB, Mrs. Willan, Frizley Old Hall, Bradford.

THE ALSATIAN CLUB, R. Barnes, 18 Queen Anne's Gate, S.W.

THE BRITISH BEDLINGTON TERRIER CLUB, Mrs. Mead, Red House, Scarborough.

THE BRITISH BULLDOG CLUB, Clem Wood, 153 Belle Vue Road, Leeds.

THE BULLDOG CLUB, T. R. Boulton, 48 Glencoe Avenue, Seven Kings.

THE BULL TERRIER CLUB, A. J. Harrison, St. Fagan's Cottage, Manor Way, Beckenham.

THE CAIRN TERRIER CLUB, Rev. T. W. L. Caspersz, Turville Heath, Henley-on-Thames.

THE CHINESE CHOW CLUB, Miss Merrett, 59 Davies Street, W.1.

THE COCKER SPANIEL CLUB, H. S. Lloyd, Swakeley's Farm, Ickenham, Middlesex.

THE DACHSHUND CLUB, Major P. C. G. Hayward, Longueville, Needham Market.

THE DEERHOUND CLUB, The Misses H. and M. Loughrey, Rosslyn, Londonderry.

THE ENGLISH SETTER CLUB, G. S. Lowe, Staplehurst Lodge, Milton Regis, Kent.

THE FIELD SPANIEL SOCIETY, R. Kelland, 105B Station Street, Birmingham.

THE FLAT-COATED RETRIEVER ASSOCIATION, Major P. C. G. Hayward, Longueville, Needham Market.

THE FOX TERRIER CLUB, N. Dawson, Bevis Marks House, E.C.

THE FRENCH BULLDOG CLUB, Mrs. Matthews, Lyndhurst, Pyrland Road, Richmond.

The Greyhound Club, W. E. Alcock, The Atlas Kennels, 88 Chancery Lane, W.C.

The Griffons Bruxellois Club, Mrs. Knapp, 10 Broadway Avenue, St. Margarets, Twickenham.

The Irish Terrier Club, Oliver Hamlin, Bellingdon, Chorley Wood, Herts.

The Irish Wolfhound Club, K. B. Strohmenger, 15 Grosvenor Gardens, S.W.1.

The Japanese Chin Club, W. H. Dowling, 20 Campden House, Peel Street, Kensington, W.

The Keeshond Club, Mrs. G. Wingfield-Digby, Sherborne Castle, Sherborne.

The Kerry Blue Terrier Club, J. W. Cummings, Fernleigh, Victoria Road, Romford.

The King Charles Spaniel Club, Mrs. Knapp, 10 Broadway Avenue, St. Margarets, Twickenham.

The Labrador Club, Mrs. Quintin Dick, 28 St. James's Place, S.W.

The London Chow Club, W. S. Lewis, 45 Rosebery Avenue, E.C.

The London and Provincial Collie Club, C. H. Pike, 89 Stoke Newington Road, N.16.

The London and Provincial Irish Terrier Club, H. Knapp, 10 Broadway Avenue, St. Margarets, Twickenham.

The London and Provincial Pekingese Club, Mrs. Knapp, 10 Broadway Avenue, St. Margarets, Twickenham.

The Newfoundland Club, Lt.-Col. W. A. Wetman, Ashley Grove, Worksop, Notts.

The North of England Dalmatian Club, G. A. C. Bury, 8 Allandale, Squire's Gate, Blackpool.

The Old English Sheepdog Club, Miss Palmer, Coney Close, St. Nicholas, Birchington, Kent.

The Papillon Club, Mrs. Knapp, 10 Broadway Avenue, St. Margarets, Twickenham.

The Pekingese Club, Mrs. L. L. Templeton, 43 Gunterstone Road, W.14.

The Pomeranian Club, Mrs. Parker, The Bungalow, Manor Road, Richmond.

The St. Bernard Club, J. Redwood, Whittington, near Oswestry.

The Saluki or Gazelle Club, Mrs. G. M. Lance, Wentfield, Wrotham.

The Schepperke Club, Mrs. Hirst, Quarry Cottage, Claverton Down, Bath.

The Scottish Dandie Dinmont Terrier Club, R. Ralston, Calderbraes, Uddingston.

The Scottish Terrier Club, Mrs. D. S. Caspersz, Turville Heath, Henley-on-Thames.

The Sealyham Terrier Club, Fred. W. Lewis, Sealyham House, Haverfordwest.

The Shetland Sheepdog Club, E. C. Pierce, 55 Parkside, Eltham, S.E.9.

The Skye and Clydesdale Terrier Club, Lady Alexander, Faygate, Sussex.

The Southern Old English Sheepdog Club, H. Knapp, 10 Broadway Avenue, St. Margarets, Twickenham.

The Welsh Corgi Club, Capt. G. Checkland Williams, The Treasury, St. Davids.

The Welsh Springer Spaniel Club, Lt.-Col. J. Downes-Powell, Artillery House, Penarth.

The Welsh Terrier Club, W. H. Brady, Glan-y-Coed, Penmaenmawr.

The West Highland White Terrier Club, J. Lee, Maulden Lodge, near Ampthill.

The Whippet Club, Capt. W. Lewis Renwick, Portfield House, Cardiff Dock.

The Wire Fox Terrier Association, H. A. W. Simmonds, The Plain, Epping, Essex.

The Yorkshire Terrier Club, J. Dunman, 7 Durand Gardens, S.W.9.

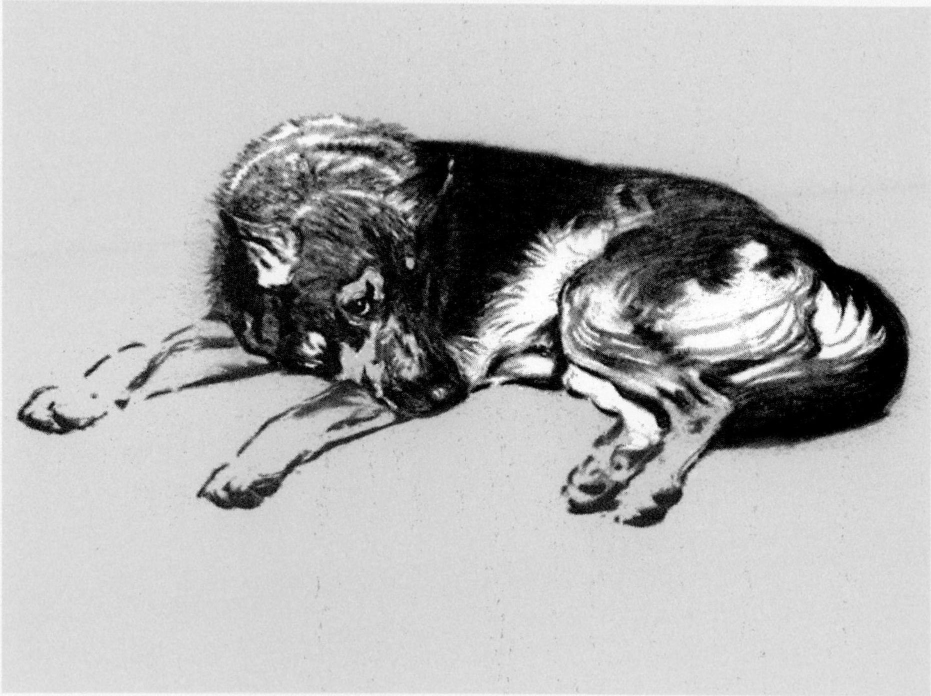